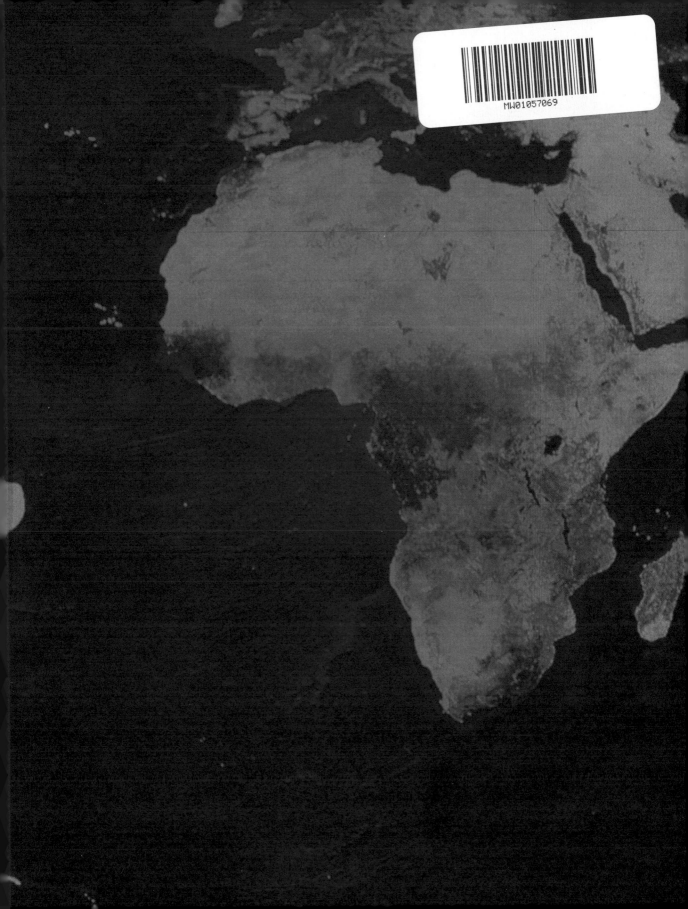

MW01057069

HumanKind

Tom Bernardin + Mark Tutssel

powerHouse Books Brooklyn, NY

This is not about advertising

This is about people

Foreword

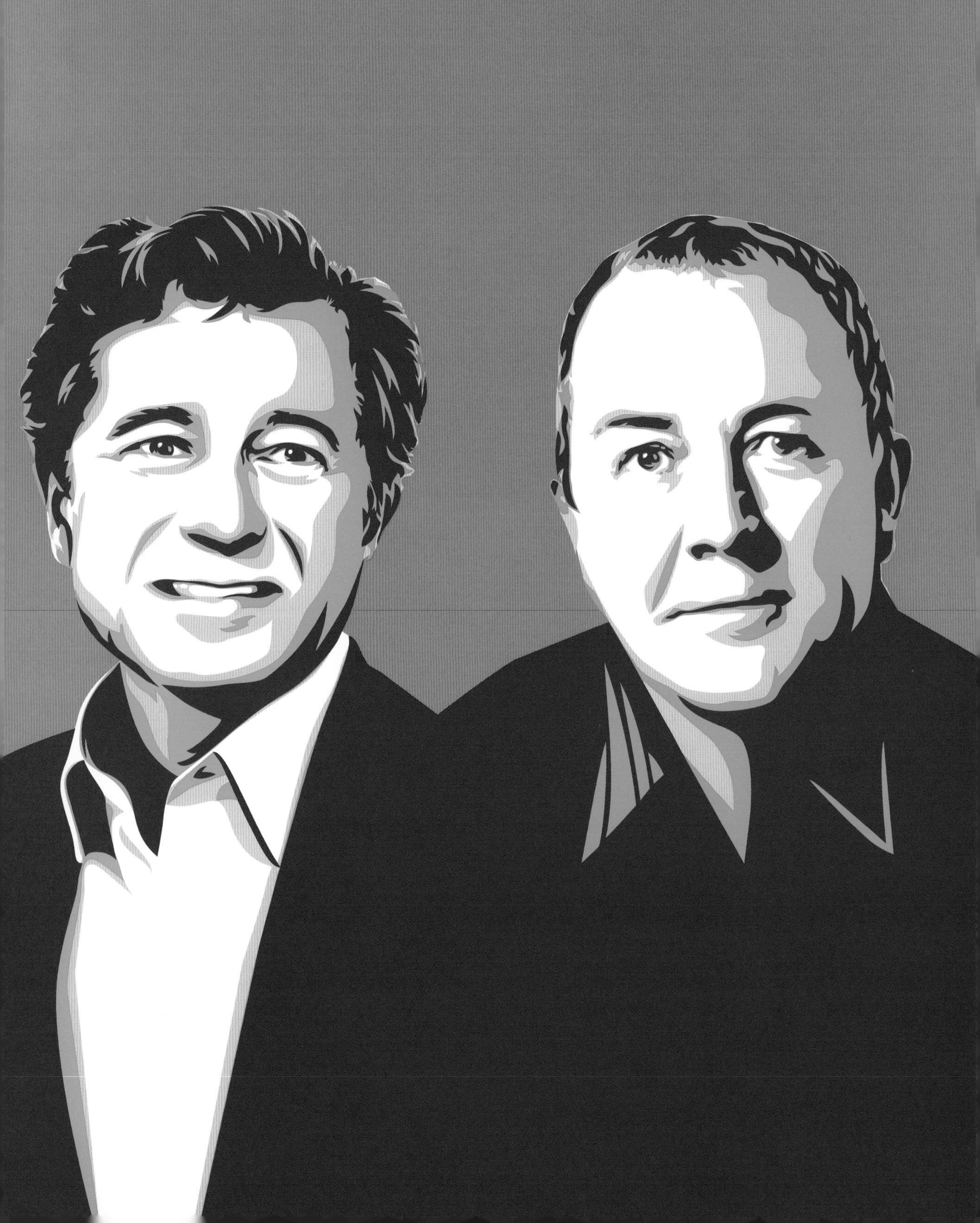

HumanKind is not about advertising or brand propositions or selling products, but a story about people, purpose, and changing behavior. It's a look at marketing that serves true human needs and not the other way around.

Everything in this business can be distilled down to two things, people and their behavior. We must never lose sight of the most important thing: what matters to people. That's why everything we do for brands is designed with a human purpose in mind. A brand without purpose is one that will never be understood or embraced by people.

Brands need to be agents of change if they're to have a role in the world. And they need to be dynamic if they're to stimulate top-line growth. So they need a point of view – a set of convictions – about how they believe the world should be. Convictions give a brand an enduring and consistent purpose. Ultimately, there are just two questions to ask to define your brand's purpose. What do you believe? And what are you going to do about it?

HumanKind is rapidly becoming a global movement, a shared belief that creativity has the power to transform human behavior. The best stories in advertising do more than turn campaigns into press releases. The brands with the best stories get to play a long-term role in people's lives, acting as a badge, a community, an entertainer, and an information resource. A brand is not made just by the people who buy it, but by the people who know about it.

HumanKind – the approach and this book – invites you into the world of Leo Burnett, a behind-the-scenes look at a global creative network that believes modern-day communication needs to be rooted in a fundamental human need. HumanKind puts laser sharp focus on the infinite power of imagination and its ability to change the way people think, feel, and ultimately, behave.

HumanKind inspires and moves people. HumanKind has the potential to change the world.

Tom Bernardin
Chairman and CEO
Leo Burnett Worldwide

Mark Tutssel
Chief Creative Officer
Leo Burnett Worldwide

About
People
Purpose
Participation
Populism
&

Creativity has the power to transform human behavior

EARTH
HOUR

Perhaps you were among the up to one billion people – that is, among the one of every seven people on the entire planet (pause right here and think about that: one of every seven people on the entire planet) who, on March 28, 2009, whether you were in New York, Paris, Bora Bora, Tunis, Dubrovnik, Montreal, San Francisco, Hanoi City, Oslo, Nairobi, Abu Dhabi, Caracas, Osaka, Nome, Haifa, a remote albatross sanctuary 800 kilometers east of Christ Church, a swarming megalopolis like Chongqing in western China, or almost anywhere else on earth, turned off the lights for an hour as part of Earth Hour, the largest mass-participation event since the dawn of time (pause right here and think about that: *since the dawn of time*), as a way of "voting" for the earth in the first-ever global "election" between the earth and global warming, to show the world that people everywhere, no matter their race, religion, gender, economic status, caste, color, or creed, can come together to create change.

Or perhaps you were one of the 34 million people who pass through Piccadilly Circus in London every year who stood just so, with your arms in the air, about 150 feet in front of the giant McDonald's billboard and had your picture taken, which because of the way the photo on the billboard in the background was positioned, made it look as if you were balancing a pigeon on your head or holding a bouquet of flowers or an umbrella in the air to ward off the drizzle.

Then again, maybe, just like thousands and thousands of parents across the United States, you sat one night with your 16-year-old child who'd just passed his or her driver's license test and discussed how to avoid being one of the almost 6,000 American teenagers who die in car crashes every year, using the Allstate teen driving contract you found online as both motivation for the talk and guide for how to have it.

Or possibly you were one of the hundreds of thousands of Romanians who signed a petition sponsored by Bergenbier calling on the country's legislature to make May 5 "Man's Day," an official holiday complete with a day off from work and worry; or among those tourists and residents in Lisbon who roamed the streets of the city's edgy Bairro Alto, São Bento, and Amoreiras neighborhoods, site of Pampero rum's Museu Efémero, a "museum without borders" that showcased the areas' best outdoor art and graffiti and went on to become a global model of urban art awareness and preservation; or a racer wannabe who became part of an Italian cultural phenomenon by posting a video of yourself on the Fiat Web site executing sharp turns at mock mach speed in an example of "air driving," the automobile equivalent of playing air guitar.

If you are a member of humankind, chances are that you have participated in one of these acts – or the scores of others that we at Leo Burnett call HumanKind acts – and have started or deepened your relationship

with these brands in the process. Earth Hour could have been communicated globally through a PSA – you know, the planet is in peril and you need to do your part to stave off all hell from breaking loose – but instead it became a global act, one that didn't just speak to people but invited them to act with purpose and actually *do something* about climate change. It was relevant. It was compelling. And up to one out of every seven people on earth thought so, too.

Similarly, if you took home a picture of yourself from Piccadilly Circus, your experience with McDonald's may not have included a hamburger and fries, but something more valuable. You experienced a moment of simple, easy enjoyment and McDonald's deepened its relationship with someone who cares enough about the brand to take a picture, create a memory, and participate in the brand's communications. McDonald's invited you into its brand and you, in turn, invited McDonald's into your life. The billboard wasn't an ad, it was an invitation to act – to participate in a HumanKind act – and to engage with the brand. It wasn't trying to sell you anything. It was just trying to connect with you. And connect it did.

HumanKind breaks the routine into which the advertising industry fell during the let-the-good-times-roll years of the late-20th and early-21st century global economic boom (and to which many people in the industry still adhere). People then had money to burn – or they could easily borrow the money to burn. Merchandise and services were flying off shelves. We were generating a need for products whose only purpose was to placate clients and shareholders' desire for more, more, more. Creativity rooted in genuine human need was devalued. In its place "positioning" began to masquerade as creativity.

Because of all of this, many of us who market brands – and if you're reading this book, that may mean you – got lazy and began to forget that it's people who make the difference. We found ways to communicate based on *our* needs and ambitions. People? Who are they?

Empty at its core, faithless to human needs, and untrue to the world in which we live, this sort of creativity sputtered and finally lost its power.

The Internet had a lot to do with this, of course. People today are savvier yet more cynical – savvier because information is literally at our fingertips, more cynical because information is literally at our fingertips. People have gone from passive to empowered, from one-size-fits-all to wanting and expecting everything to be custom-made, from inferred knowledge to direct knowledge.

We are no longer "consumers" first, but humans first.

As humans, we are reevaluating everything because we can. If technology exists to let us better know ourselves and the world around us, to form new insights, to go physically, mentally, psychically, intellectually, creatively, and imaginatively where no one has ever gone before, then it's in our human nature to go there, and go there soon. There's no use fighting it. We are explorers.

As humans, we have changed our behavior in relation to the world as surely as the world has changed. And as marketers we must make a corresponding shift in order to stay relevant or we will shift to irrelevance faster than the Wicked Witch of the West melted when Dorothy doused her with water. The only problem is, how?

We can no longer build brands, we can only move people. We can no longer position brands, we can only create content that encourages authentic conversations between people and brands based on a brand's human purpose. We can no longer rely on ads that speak *to* people, we must provide people with opportunities to act. As marketers, we can no longer claim that it is up to us to be the motor that drives brands, we can only empower people and let them take the steering wheel themselves.

That's why this book – filled as it is with extraordinary examples of Leo Burnett's HumanKind approach to communications – is really about people, about you, and us, and everyone who makes up the human race. For without people, purpose, and participation, none of this would matter. A billion people would not have turned off their lights on March 28, 2009.

HumanKind responds to a world that sometimes seems inhuman and unkind. Not "kind" as in altruistic – though sometimes it definitely is – but as in respectful.

Work created through a HumanKind lens respects people's needs, ambitions, intelligence, sense of humor, enjoyment of life, understanding of life's opportunities and limitations, and, perhaps most of all, in a world in which so many of us never seem to be able to fit in everything we want to do, it respects people's time. It rewards people for the time they spend with our communication.

Inherent in the definition of HumanKind is a deep understanding of and sensitivity to what it means to be human, to be a person, first and foremost – whether a father or mother, teen or tween, Laplander or Lett, African or African-American, yoga instructor or bocce ball player, clarinetist or bricklayer, brussels sprout farmer or high-powered CEO, male or female, gay or straight, redhead or blonde.

At Leo Burnett, we've thought really hard about this because the values initially brought to this company by its founder, Leo Burnett, continue to run in our veins. HumanKind reaffirms the basic principles upon which Leo Burnett the man founded Leo Burnett the company in the first place.

Leo Burnett was a man who did things his own way, a plainspoken Midwesterner, a man rarely seen without a cigarette in his mouth, a man who chose to make the apple his corporate symbol after a Chicago newspaper columnist said that his agency, founded during the Great Depression, would fail and that he'd soon be on the street

The work of an advertising agency is warmly and immediately human. It deals with needs, wants, dreams, and hopes. Its 'product' cannot be turned out on an assembly line.

Leo Burnett

selling apples like every other poor *schmo*. A man who had no use for long, polysyllabic words or complicated ideas that stood for nothing but being polysyllabic and complicated. Leo Burnett died in 1971, but his values and the emphasis he placed on creativity as not just *a* but *the* driving force in advertising live on in every one of the more than 90 offices worldwide that today bear his name.

Leo Burnett was somebody who, as a practitioner, recognized the paramount importance of people – and ensured that his agency's respect for people and its curiosity about them was always palpable.

Given this, not surprisingly, the Leo Burnett company developed into an agency that at its best worked with clients who owned big brands with mainstream appeal and large audiences. It created for those brands big, accessible ideas whose power was in their size and accessibility and their infectious, mnemonic energy, what Leo Burnett called "big, enduring ideas." The Marlboro Man, the Jolly Green Giant, Tony the Tiger, the Pillsbury Doughboy.

HumanKind is true to Leo Burnett's original vision and values because it drives us to continue to create the kind of awe-inspiring, innovative work that built the agency's legacy without letting that legacy dictate the future. It takes into account a faster-paced, more competitive and more complex world than our founder could have foreseen.

HumanKind, as an approach, is honest, transparent, and authentic; it respects people; it intuitively responds to their thirst for creativity and imagination and connection; and, finally, it drives the belief that creativity has the power to transform human behavior and lives. **We focus on ideas and acts that become part of the social fabric.**

It's no longer enough for marketers to be impressive but distant; people must be at the heart of every piece of communication we as marketers create. In other words, we have to let people into the moment – and act – of communication. The experience has to add something to people's lives in order for people to value it. If communication is trying to change human behavior, the communication itself needs to be located within that behavior. You can't say, well, we'll change human behavior but our communication just won't relate to that behavior in any way. Increasingly, communication that works, such as the McDonald's billboards at Piccadilly Circus, is communication that is wired into behavior – it inhabits it.

Leo Burnett's entire global network is using HumanKind as a compass point, and this shared focus gives us a common way to see ourselves and an effective means to evaluate our work. After all, everything in this industry boils down to two things: people and behavior. So the starting point is always going to be people.

We are the ultimate people watchers.

Our job is to move people emotionally. Sure, you can underpin the job with rational reasons – our clients' functional benefits – but ultimately our job is to create a lifelong emotional relationship with people. You keep that lifelong emotional relationship when you find a true human purpose behind a brand with which you cannot disagree and you feed and celebrate it in human and imaginative ways.

HumanKind speaks to the world we live in today – with all its glorious confusion, beauty, technology, and wonder. It is an approach to marketing that says yes, marketing can serve the true needs of people and not the other way around. And here's how.

People want to be offered more interaction with brands they care about. They want to be allies not targets. They want the opportunity to actively test brand promises not just receive brand promises. They want the power to speak openly and loudly about their experience with a brand. And we as a company have taken that on.

We can return marketing to that nobler thing and, in a way, that's the essence of HumanKind.

To experience the richness and diversity of the Leo Burnett team's understanding of HumanKind, we asked people in all our offices worldwide to interpret HumanKind through photography. We then matched their pictures with our own words to create a unified and universal expression of HumanKind. See these original photographs on pages 15 through 47.

HumanKind is rooted
in human understanding

HumanKind doesn't interrupt people, it involves them

HumanKind aims to add something to people's lives

HumanKind doesn't ask people to care, it invites them to participate

HumanKind is focused on human behavior change

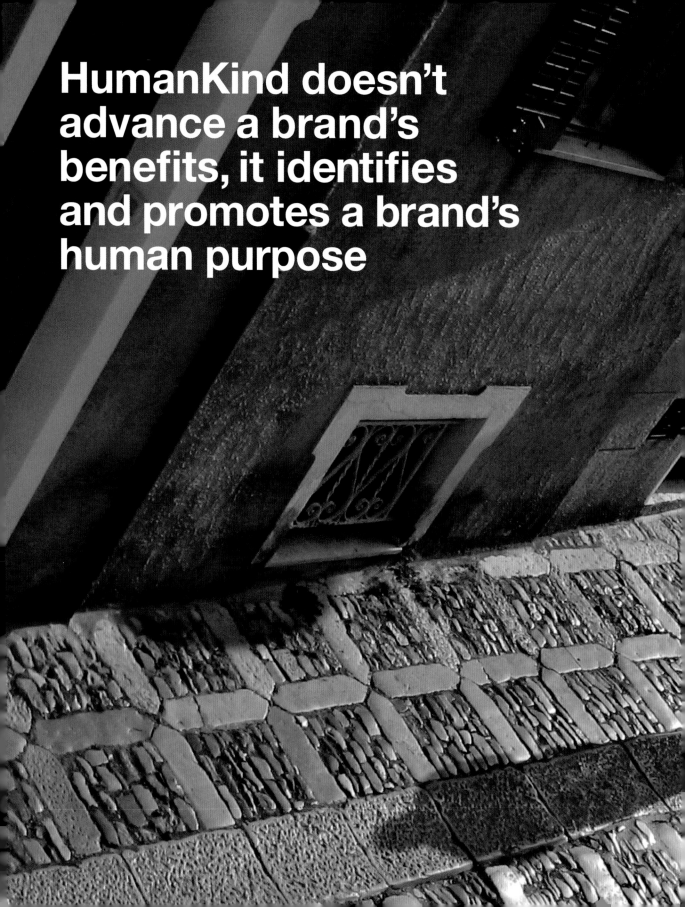

HumanKind doesn't advance a brand's benefits, it identifies and promotes a brand's human purpose

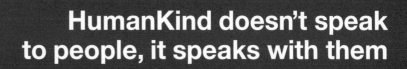

**HumanKind doesn't speak
to people, it speaks with them**

HumanKind doesn't demand people's attention, it respects it and rewards it

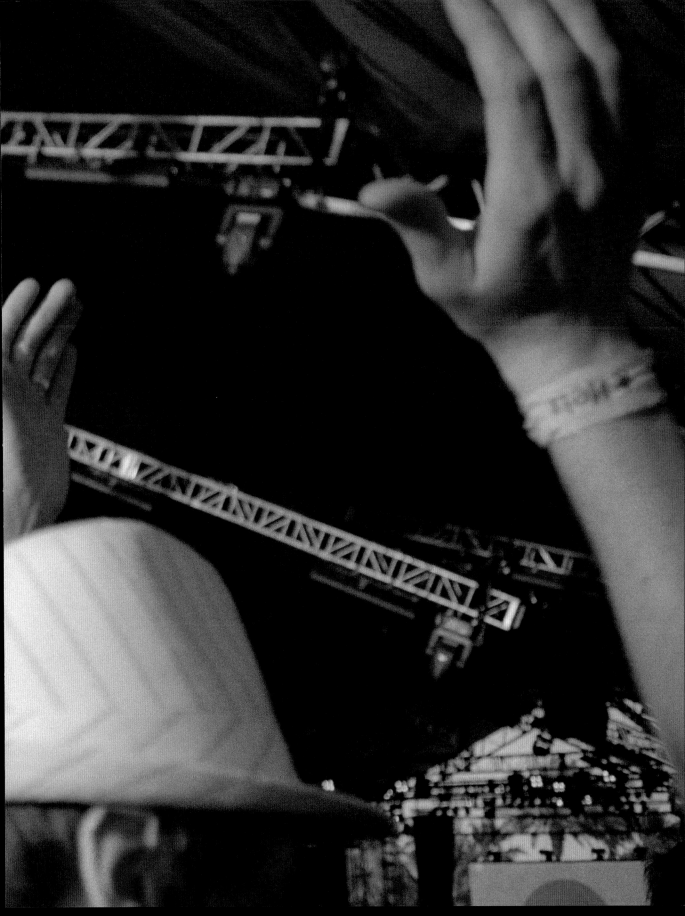

HumanKind has real experiential value at the time that it's consumed rather than just dispensing a message

HumanKind doesn't make people empty, short-term promises. It encourages authentic,

emotional, long-term relationships between brands and the people who use them

HumanKind grows deep from within humanity and responds naturally to people's individual, unique need to make the world a better place, to make their own lives a more personally fulfilling experience, or even to just make the moment, the here and now, a more humane, pleasant, passing of time

Ultimately, HumanKind is "populist" – when successful it can uniquely unify broad populations of people with big, accessible, likable, and visible ideas

And our brand of creativity, which changes human behavior and results in this sort of popularity – this HumanKind populism – proves that HumanKind works

People, purpose, participation, and populism

Welcome to a book about HumanKind

Measuring HumanKind

Number crunch: We judge our work against HumanKind standards on a one to ten scale

You're in Milan – say you're meandering along Via Montenapoleone and the narrow side streets that branch off it, passing Giorgio Armani, Dolce & Gabbana, Buccellati, Fornasetti, and all the other shops whose windows glisten with clothes, jewels, and objets d'art. An especially fetching pair of shoes catches your eyes. You look at the price tag and see that what you have in your bank account won't cover it, at least not if you plan to pay your rent and eat for the next three months. You could put the shoes on your credit card but then you'd be shelling out even more as you pay for those shoes month by month. Imagine if a painless way existed to save for the shoes on your own schedule *and* earn interest at the same time. Imagine if that savings plan took about 12 seconds to set up and you could do it all from your phone.

With prompting from Leo Burnett in Milan, that's exactly what the e-bank ING agreed to develop – a mobile phone application and a browser plug-in that help people instantly create savings accounts for things they want to buy instead of instantly handing over their well-worn charge card.

Rather than plunging into debt to buy the shoes – let's just say it's a pair of shoes from Fratelli Rossetti – the ING phone app enables you to take a snapshot of the product's bar code. The bank, which has no brick and mortar branches, will then automatically open a savings account for the shoes. You can customize the length of time in which you plan to save money for the shoes and funds will automatically be diverted from your checking account into the new Fratelli Rossetti savings account until you have enough money to buy them.

A modern-day layaway plan, yes, but this layaway plan doesn't just exist waiting to be funded. Rather, it works to motivate people to save, gently teaching them about money management. It *involves* them. It's a future-facing idea that helps a client develop lifelong relationships with people – and an incredibly useful contemporary tool that has the potential to fundamentally change the way people handle their money. Better yet, it's the kind of *category-defying* act that best illustrates the power and point of HumanKind: It speaks to how people live today, it changes how people live today, and it adds something infinitely good to people's lives today. In other words, it puts people at the heart of the brand's communication.

HumanKind provides the context to produce category-defying work

We like the phrase "category-defying." We like that it implies not only a new way of thinking, but also a new way of being, a new way of applying creativity, a new way of behaving. Communications that are category-defying can be inspired only by ideas that spring from understanding people – how they live and what they need to realize their dreams. It's this kind of thinking and understanding and application that will compel attention, Induce participation, and give people the opportunity to build and sustain people's brands.

1 2 3
4 5 6
7+8 9
10

HumanKind gives marketers the freedom to do what's best for people, which ultimately is what's best for their clients' brands.

The ING campaign is a fantastic example of HumanKind. You feel it in your bones. But how do you really know? What criteria are we judging it against?

This is where our Global Product Committee comes into play. At its most prosaic, GPC is a measurement tool that allows us to put some definition around how we talk about work and judge its success. But we don't think of GPC as prosaic at all (though the phrase "measurement tool" is).

In fact, it's the exact opposite. It is dynamic, insightful, constructive, instructive, and real. A management resource that allows us to assess our creative teams and see which need a shot of adrenaline and which are working at their best, "GPC" is also how we refer to our quarterly meetings – "the GPC meeting." It's here where the agency's top 25 or so creative thinkers come together somewhere in the world – over the past several years we have met in Bangkok, Shanghai, Istanbul, Toronto, Buenos Aries, Mexico City, London, Melbourne, and Madrid – to review hundreds of pieces of work, piece by piece by piece.

**Every print ad.
Every television commercial.
Every event.
Every product design.
Every short film.
Every integrated campaign.
Every social media creation.
Every innovative idea.**

Everything created during the previous quarter that was in some way a part of a client campaign, a part of a brand's potential interaction with its audience.

Each is viewed, discussed, and scored on a scale of 1 – 10 on hand-held meters. Scores are announced. A piece of work, and by association the teams that created it and the office in which those teams work, are part of this judgment process. No one is spared. But no one is persecuted, either. In fact, experience shows just the opposite. Whether an individual or team or office receives kudos or not, almost to a person we hear that the GPC meetings energize them, further educate them on HumanKind, and motivate them to bring HumanKind to their work. People leave more excited than ever.

Yes, our Global Product Committee – known around the agency simply as GPC – is, like any committee or process, at any company anywhere, an internal contrivance. It exists within our walls and minds. And yes, GPC in all its dimension, is something that we use to judge ourselves, and yes, we are only human, and yes, in some cases, we may misjudge ourselves and our work. But marketing is an imperfect science (hell *science* is an imperfect science) and the GPC is an attempt, a very good attempt, at measuring and self-evaluating our work so we can produce better work. HumanKind work.

These quarterly events are crucial to HumanKind's success not just as an approach, but as a day-to-day way of performing, defining our culture, and ensuring that marketing stays relevant even as the world changes, technology advances, and people's attention and interests evolve.

GPC takes the theory behind HumanKind and makes it real – in some cases, actually touchable, tastable, smellable, seeable, and hearable. It helps us focus our thinking and refine our creative executions. It lets us say yes, HumanKind is working and…

This. Is. What. It. Is.

It's no longer enough to just take a serious look at our work or to have regular review sessions where people support and praise and promote creative output or express doubt and criticize and quibble over it. Without a well-defined, agreed-upon global standard, creative reviews are merely conversations that hang in the air like dust. The results of our GPC meetings are shared with our clients, who together with us then have a point of reference to use that promotes frank discussion, sometimes some uncomfortable moments and pregnant pauses, and other times more ideas and inspiration.

The GPC actually has been around longer than HumanKind. But when we began to evolve into a HumanKind company, we looked at the scale and realized it no longer worked for where we were as an agency and where, more importantly, we were going. So we rethought the criteria by which we judge our work around the world. We had to if HumanKind was to be our future and take hold throughout every office. And today the GPC scale used to measure the success of our work as it expresses the HumanKind ideal is exactly right.

To be considered an expression of HumanKind, work must score at least a 7 – in other words, what we call a 7+. We'll get to that in a minute.

Simply put, work scored a one, two, three, or four are failures.

At the low end of this low group, a one implies not just a lack of success, but almost a willful disservice to the people who make up our clients' teams, to the brands, to our company, and to people. People everywhere, whether they see or experience the work or not. Why? Because it diminishes people as humans. It underscores their worst perceptions of our industry. And it lessens their receptiveness to future communications – not just from a specific brand, but from brands overall.

Two isn't much better. Work deemed a two is like an interior monologue. It's a brand talking to itself about itself for itself. It offers nothing outside itself. It's selfish.

A score of three is interesting only because so much of the work out in the world would fall here if all that work were evaluated closely and with patience, concern, and creativity. We call this work "invisible" advertising and it's probably 80 percent to 90 percent of what communication is today. Despite how much there is, you never see it, you never hear it, you never consume it. It's wallpaper. By HumanKind standards, work regarded as a three assumes it has a divine right to people's attention, that people will connect with whatever communication is thrown their way. That's not only wrong, it's insulting to people. People are not interested in advertising for advertising's sake. Today we simply must reward people for the time they spend with our communications.

Ah, four. We don't like a four. Ever. A four is a puzzlement. It's close but no cigar. It's looking at a piece of communication and knowing intuitively that whoever created it didn't ask crucial questions: What is this brand representing in society? What is its point of difference? What is its point of view? What's its personality? What is this brand *about*?

The answers to these questions are the keys that unlock the door of creativity because they force you to investigate and evaluate the purpose of the brand, not the proposition, not the rational reason to believe, but the purpose – what value the brand creates in a person's life. And that's the most important thing.

Once you have a brilliant brand purpose, how then do you use the power of creativity to amplify it and activate it through a range of contact points? And that is the idea itself. A purpose is a purpose; a purpose isn't an idea alone, no matter how creative. With a purpose, the hard part finally begins because a purpose will give you a spring board into something fresh and something new.

Think of a brand proposition – its benefits, its technical superiority, its advantages – like a diving platform a few meters off the ground. There's only one way you can go off of it: out and down. It's rock solid, it's rational, there's consensus. Everyone buys into it.

Out. Down. Done.

Now think what happens when you have an authentic human brand purpose that elevates the platform and turns it into a vibrant springboard. All of a sudden, the world of possibilities opens up. You're now in a world of imagination that gives you the freedom to think in a different way, where you are allowed to go out and down if you want, but also up, this way, that way, somersault, flip, sideways – in any of a million and one directions in your search for an idea that soars. You have the freedom to find the idea that really does bring the brand purpose to life in the most imaginative way.

Work nearing or at five starts to glimmer with possibility. While still not rising to the HumanKind ideal, it embodies an authentic human brand purpose, a purpose that can be intuited by people, that at minimum speaks to what the brand does for people.

Still, that's not good enough – not enough to move us marketers into what we earlier referred to as a nobler profession. Work veering toward six is getting warmer. It's expressing a brand purpose and doing so with an intelligent idea that respects and rewards people. And yet it only goes that far, which isn't far enough.

And seven+ our standard? Hello, gorgeous.

Seven+ is an obviously brilliant idea executed with heart in an original fashion and crafted to perfection. What "acts, not ads" challenges you to do is activate and amplify a brand purpose in the most imaginative way, to invite participation in the brand, to give people what they need in their life. When you do that – when you allow a brand to do that – people, on their own, begin to create great brands, great people's brands. They create, in HumanKind parlance, populism.

Eight – we call it the 8 ball – is that magical idea that encompasses the ideals of HumanKind. The important distinction – and its importance can't be overstated – is that this 8 ball work has the ability to change behavior, not only to celebrate the brand purpose but to actually create change, to

Teams that produce 8 ball-worthy work get an actual eight ball to prove they know how to change human behavior.

change the way people think and feel about something. Not only is it a brilliant idea rooted in a brilliant brand purpose, a meaningful purpose, and executed to perfection, but it's an idea that's so big it has that ability to connect on a much bigger scale.

And there's an effect: you've changed behavior. No small thing. ING's savings phone app garnered an 8 ball.

But if getting over the hump from three to four and then four to five and subsequently five to six and six to seven+ is a challenge, the gulf between eight and nine is as big as all of them put together.

Nine changes not just how we behave momentarily or in the short-term, but it literally changes the way we live. And this work is obviously rare. In fact, though we have created and continue to create extraordinary seven+ work across the globe, nine is so rare that we can point only to Earth Hour. It was a piece of communication that really united the planet, that united humankind around a common goal, around a common purpose. And how often can you say that about anything?

When up to one in seven of the global population acts in the same exact way at the same exact moment in time, it's a remarkable feat. It turned Earth Hour into the fastest growing brand in the world. It's the biggest-ever interaction between a brand and humankind in the history of humankind. It was visionary, brave, and deeply rooted in the brand's human purpose.

Ten is probably the easiest one to define: It doesn't just change how people act or how people live, it changes *the world*. Simply put, only God has created a ten.

Destructive

overheard at Milan GPC

1.4

This is a complete waste of money. It pollutes the public space. Work that scores this low requires an intervention, and possibly re-staffing the team that produced it.

No Idea

overheard at Chicago GPC
2.7
There's no substance here, no creativity, and no apparent effort to craft something that holds people's interest. Work that is this appallingly uninteresting does a disservice to our industry.

Invisible

overheard at London GPC
3.3
This work assumes it has
a divine right to people's
attention. It doesn't. No
one will notice it. There is
nothing here to capture
or engage interest. This is
formulaic, predictable, and
instantly forgettable.

I Don't Know What This Brand Stands For

overheard at Toronto GPC
4.5
This is cliche, and
there's nothing here that
distinguishes this brand
from the others in the
category. There's nothing
distinctive here.

I Understand the Brand's Purpose

overheard at Bangkok GPC

5.4

The brand's purpose is
clear, and you've conveyed
a message about what
this product offers people.
The art direction could be
refined and the copy could
be distilled further.

An Intelligent Idea

overheard at Buenos Aires GPC

6.7

An intriguing execution that captures people's interest. This is a solid campaign idea, the art direction is eye-catching, and you're inviting people in. An idea that treats people with intelligence and invites them into the brand.

A HumanKind Act

7.4

This is executed beautifully
around a strong idea. You're
conveying a product truth in a
way that creates engagement
and entertainment for people.
The crafting is exquisite
and the attention to detail
is masterful.

Changes the Way People Think and Feel

overheard at Melbourne GPC
8.1
This is a brilliant way to
involve people in a powerful
brand story, and you've used
a compelling insight to really
hold people's interest. We
love how you've deftly woven
this communication into the
social fabric, and it's perfectly
amplified and activated
for maximum impact.

Changes the Way People Live

overheard at Istanbul GPC
discussing the
2009 Earth Hour campaign
This campaign embodies
everything we value about
communication — it's
hugely ambitious, brilliantly
crafted, and compels people
to participate through
messages that captivate
people's imagination.
This is visionary work!

10

People

We are eternal students of human behavior

Everything in this business comes down to two things: people and their behavior. We can look at a business problem as a set of numbers. Or we can look at it through a more human lens. By looking through a human lens, we can change how people feel, think, and behave using the power of creativity.

Understanding people and their behavior is the only thing that matters. It allows us to *discover* fundamental human needs and in turn *uncover* human truths. It inspires us to *recover* a brand's human purpose. If we understand people, we will get to purpose. Purpose then leads us to participation, which, if fully realized, results in HumanKind's ultimate goal, brand populism.

Without people – and without insisting that our teams become eternal students of human behavior – HumanKind could not, would not and, frankly, should not, exist.

This may sound obvious, but it needs to be said so there's no confusion. We're talking about *people* and their behavior, not about "consumers," a word that *implies* people yet simultaneously suggests some other life form.

We do not believe in consumers; we believe in people.

We do not research, observe, and study consumers; we research, observe, and study people.

We do not talk to, interact with, and otherwise build relationships with consumers; we do these things with people.

If you think of people as consumers, your communications with them will remain as inauthentic as the word itself. But if you think of people as people, and create advertising through that lens, you have a shot at creating work that speaks to human needs and desires.

To create HumanKind communications, you must first understand humankind. And that depends on people – the people we are trying to reach *and* the people at the agency creating the work. HumanKind thrives in an atmosphere where people are encouraged and rewarded for seeking to know more.

At Leo Burnett, we glean insight from our people *and* from our clients around the globe whose intelligence, curiosity, creativity, articulateness, and even obsessiveness drive them to think hard about human behavior, motivation, and development. These are people with brilliant minds who aren't embarrassed to use them, who aren't too coy to express what they think, who aren't so shy that they let false (or even real) modesty get in the way of seriously deep thinking and commanding insight.

Sometimes their thinking is big, broad, and limitless. What is the meaning of life? Why do we sometimes share, sometimes covet, and other times hoard? Why do we love and hate? Why do we sometimes love and hate the same person? And how is it possible to love and hate the same person at the very same moment?

But other times their thinking is granular and acutely focused, drilling down deeper and deeper to reach some essential, indisputable human truth.

We embrace not one way of thinking –
the big and wide or the deep and narrow –
but as many ways as possible to ensure
that our understanding of what makes people
people and the changing nature of what
makes people people is always evolving,
growing, surprising, motivating, alluring,
and provocative.

It's not merely that we want to know
everything, but that we have a ceaseless
urge to know more.

The more we know, the more we want to know.

The more we want to know, the more questions we ask.

The more questions we ask, the more we devise ways to ask them.

The more we devise ways to ask questions, the more people we come into contact with.

The more people we come into contact with, the more information we gather.

The more information we gather, the more generalizations we form.

The more generalizations we form, the more we realize that we need to know more to move beyond generalizations to specifics.

And soon we run out of breath because
our quest is endless because we can never
know everything – and besides, everything
keeps changing! – even though everything,
at least everything up to and including this
very nanosecond, is what we want to know.

This relentless exploration has led to all
sorts of discoveries into what people think
and how they live.

Every other year in Russia, for instance,
our team there – with the help of 125 "change-
chasers" – produces a dynamic report on
the changes in and minutiae of Russian
life. Without any knowledge of our Russian
group's aptly named *Book of Change*,
our team in Saudi Arabia created the
Book of Possibilities, which offers surprising
information and insight into the evolving lives
of men, women, and children in the Middle
East (Saudi rappers and heavy metal bands,
anyone?), while in Thailand we've created an
ethnographic experience called *Dirty Feet*
that pushes teams to move beyond retail
audits, brand trackings, and other number-
crunching research. It pushes them to get
out of the office and get their feet dirty – to
unearth new insights into what people there
think, prefer, dream, desire, and need. And
in Japan, our annual *BeaconEye* delivers
the latest insights into this fast-moving,
technology-savvy society and what drives
its incredible appetite for newness and
innovation. Each report offers our teams and
clients heaps of insight that both lend context
to how people live moment to moment and
motivate all of us to rethink and rejuvenate
products and services – to catch the zeitgeist
and remain relevant and grow.

Deep dives into human behavior like these and the many others taking place around the world keep us in the moment. While many human characteristics remain immutable, technology and innovation have changed the very nature of what it means to be a person, how we lead our lives, and what drives, satisfies, and ultimately, moves us. Profound changes happen every day as the world expands and contracts and as the role in our lives of religion, war, money, time, family, fashion, the environment, celebrity, work, culture, the media, medicine, and science ebbs and flows.

But it's not only big, well-researched studies that can have profound influence and provide extraordinary insight.

Not too long ago several people on our Toronto creative team, while pondering ideas for the then-troubled Toronto Humane Society (THS), went to a local coffee shop. As they were deep in thought, staring out the window, one of them noticed that every time someone walked by with a dog, passers by, as well as people in the coffee shop, smiled. When you get a pet, this creative realized, especially perhaps, a pet from a humane society, it's not only the pet's life that changes, but your life too. Pets make people happy. They make us smile. Living with a pet not only changes the pet's life, but it changes its owner's life, too. "Adopt a New Life" – for a pet, for yourself – became not just a tag line for THS but a prescription for how it should think about and communicate its mission.

After becoming aware of the THS's success and the rebranding effort that preceded it,

The Alachua County (Florida) Humane Society (ACHS) contacted us for a similar rebirth. Its building, virtually a truck stop on the highway, was a sad place. It didn't just lack warmth, but optimism, too. And that same sad-sack feeling pervaded the humane society's communications and even its relationship with the surrounding community. It simply wasn't a place people wanted to be or an atmosphere in which people could imagine adding to their lives by adopting a pet. Like "Adopt a New Life," the ACHS's "A New Life Awaits" gave it a double-sided purpose that was the inspiration for it to recreate itself as a positive place that improves people's lives. As a result, denizens of Alachua County thought differently about their humane society and the widespread happiness it could bring.

Changing people's lives was also at the heart of a campaign created for the Learning and Skills Council (LSC) in England that already used the tag line, "Our future. It's in our hands." Armed with research showing a proportion of the country's population was woefully deficient in its math skills, the LSC challenged our teams to drive enrollment in basic math courses.

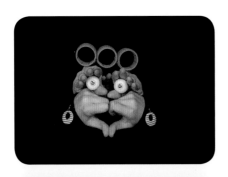

We began to talk to people and learned that their fear of math wasn't based on how they felt today, but on how they felt way back when they were first in school and learning – and failing – the basics. The group conversations felt more like therapy sessions. We realized we would need to return them to the time when things went wrong and rebuild in them the confidence they once had.

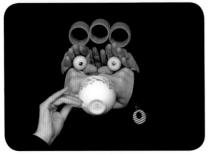

And that's how *Beryl* was born, an approachable, somewhat comic everyman (despite being a woman) literally created out of old-fashioned handwork. Beryl expressed the fear and anxiety these people felt. In turn they identified with her and were able to face their fears. Beryl's vulnerability and, eventually, her renewed confidence come through in her demeanor and words. She became a local hero, all by keying into a simple human insight.

A far less upbeat but no less honest and insightful campaign was created for the Department for Transport, also in London, after the Leo Burnett team there used the powerful – though not uncommon – insight that children learn best when you explain the reason behind what it is you are trying to teach them.

At the heart of the campaign was "The Cautionary Tale," a timeless cultural phenomenon that transcends fashion, age, and gender and speaks readily to today's savvy and precocious generation of kids. Four characters, hauntingly animated to make their injuries a focal point, told cautionary tales about different road safety behaviors: "the boy who didn't stop, look and listen," "the girl who didn't dress bright in the dark," "the boy who didn't look for a safe place to cross," and "the girl who rode her bike all wrong." All these cautionary tales played on the fascination kids have with the macabre and it changed their behavior.

the boy who didn't look for a safe place to cross:

He couldn't be bothered to walk to a place

Where cars could be seen from a nice open space

So he crossed the road right next to a bend

Now his arm, for some while, will be struggling to mend

A car cannot dodge what it cannot see

So flattened the boy (unfortunately)

Now he can't swim, dress himself or go kart

'Cause his arm is all limp and falling apart.

Always cross where you can see what's coming.

That's a fitting conclusion. When it comes to people – and a marketer's understanding of them – always cross where you can see what's coming.

Hariri Foundation Khede Kasra

In pursuing its purpose to empower women, the Beirut-based Hariri Foundation for Sustainable Human Development focused attention on the kasra, an Arabic inflection sign that appears above a word when the word is directed at men and below it when directed at women. When the kasra is omitted altogether, as in most printed material, women are excluded from the dialogue. Using a series of traditional and mobile interactive billboards in public places that said "Your right," "Your responsibility," and "Your will," Leo Burnett's "Khede Kasra" campaign (literally, "make your mark") asked women to add the kasra using stickers and other devices – some even used lipstick – to empower themselves and their gender and show that even small gestures

Your responsibility

(feminine)

can make a difference. Further introduced
through e-mail, Facebook, and YouTube;
promoted on-air by news anchors, in blogs,
and throughout the media; and endorsed
by the country's Minister of Education, the
campaign transformed a symbol of women's
inequality into one of female empowerment.

Using the kasra to educate and unite people,
and to move them to act, the campaign
reflected the HumanKind approach by using
purpose and participation to spark lasting
behavior change.

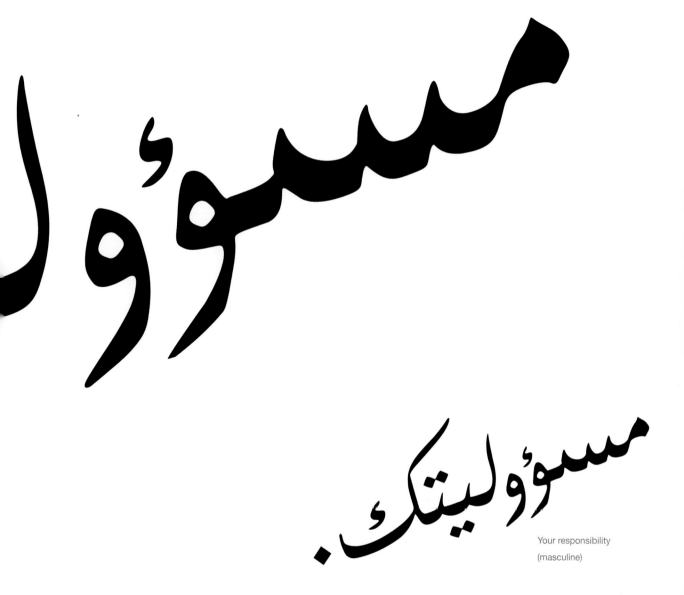

مسٶول

مسٶوليتك

Your responsibility
(masculine)

McDonald's

It's simple: The purpose of McDonald's is to create simple, easy enjoyment, and the purpose of the company's communications is to be simply and easily enjoyed. Like the brand itself, it's not complicated, there's no context, subtext, or subliminal meaning. Three simple words, one idea, that represent a human desire that McDonald's can uniquely satisfy for tens of millions of people around the world every day.

Three simple words, one idea

Simple, easy enjoyment capitalizes on a massive trend. People today crave simplicity in life. It's what people desire of McDonald's. It's the promise of an experience they want and expect to have from the moment they see the Golden Arches.

We never say the words "Simple, Easy Enjoyment" in McDonald's communication, but we certainly want people to feel it. Simply said, people should enjoy the brand every time they come into contact with it. We have to create content that people love. "I'm lovin' it" is not just an advertising slogan, it's the human reward people feel, experience, and enjoy while they spend time with the brand and our communication.

Our communications for McDonald's, whether created in the UK, like the *Everybody* spot, or in Chicago, like "Sundial," give people a reason to say "I'm lovin' it" in a fresh new way every day.

The truth about McDonald's is that everyone eats there. You can have a quick nosh or settle in and surf the Internet on your laptop. You can have dinner with your family or celebrate a special occasion with your friends. A burger and fries does it for some. A cup of coffee for others. Old and young; rich and poor; high-class or no class; laborers, loafers, and lovers; men, women, and children. Everyone has a home at McDonald's. For this beautifully written and observed slice-of-life, 60-second TV spot out of the UK, called *Everybody*, the team captured the different and diverse folks who eat at McDonald's with what can only be described as an ode to the simple, easy enjoyment people experience while there. Notice it mentions the food – brief nods to Big Macs and McNuggets – but, ultimately, it's about the role the brand plays in the lives of virtually everyone and, as important, the role people play in the life of the brand.

Now the labourers and cablers and council motion-tablers were just passing by.

And the Gothy types and scoffy types and like-their-coffee-frothy types were just passing by.

Those on their own, whilst on the phone, dunking McNuggets and having a moan, were just passing by.

The driving-thru with hungry crew who've just pulled off the A32 were just passing by. And the IT bods, with taps and prods, eating a Big Mac whilst writing their blogs, were just passing by.

And the first-in types and lurking types and like-to-lose-their-gherkin types and suddenly-just-burst-in types, were just passing by.

And the extroverts and introverts and guys in newly ironed shirts who like to text outrageous flirts, were just passing by.

And the little folk who share a joke and nudge and poke about that bloke who slurps his coke and gives his goaty beard a stroke, were just passing by.

There's a McDonald's for everyone.

BIG NOTHING

While full of heart and humanity, this spot for McDonald's is in itself 30 seconds of simple, easy enjoyment, understatedly conveying the idea that the restaurant's burgers are nothing but 100 percent beef from British and Irish farms. Called *Big Nothing* it is actually about that little something that makes McDonald's special.

PROUD PAPA

Proud Papa is a wonderful story celebrating a son's academic achievements. It's told in a highly imaginative and original way. Authentic storytelling at its very best.
Marlena Peleo-Lazar Chief Creative Officer, McDonald's

Theater of the Streets

Triple thick milkshakes

i'm lovin' it

Leo Burnett is a remarkable agency.
They create truly amazing out-of-home
for McDonald's that turns heads, wins
hearts, and moves people.

Neil Golden Chief Marketing Officer
McDonald's

P&G

It's easy to see why a company like P&G, whose overriding purpose is to improve people's lives, would want to do more than just talk about what its brands do. After all, the product categories in which its brands compete are crowded with competitors whose functions are similar (even if their effectiveness is not). As P&G works toward the idea of brand populism, uncovering and bringing to life a separate HumanKind brand purpose for each of its brands allows the brands to discover new and relevant ways of both expressing creativity and communicating about their benefits that go beyond the merely functional.

Cheer, for example, exists to make people's lives a little brighter, a double meaning referring to both the literal brightness of the clothes being washed and the brighter quality of one's life. But how about for people who wear black all the time – not a color we associate with "brightness" exactly but one that can make a black-clad person feel cool and, in turn, good about themselves? For these people there's Cheer Dark. The chubby faces of the black-clad metal kid and intellectual featured in the Cheer Dark ads, along with their significantly trimmer bodies (black is slimming, after all), tell people, "Yes, we understand why you wear dark clothes. We *get* it." In other words, use Cheer Dark and while your clothes will remain store-bought black, your life will be a little brighter.

Each of P&G's brands inhabits its own, unique human brand purpose discovered through purpose workshops and other activities – for instance, Dreft laundry detergent's human brand purpose – why it exists – is to help women look and feel beautiful, while Tampax lets women play by their own rules, Always and Whisper are devoted to helping girls embrace their womanhood positively, Max Factor believes in empowering women to feel adored, and Koleston exists to unapologetically celebrate the sensuality in every woman. Each brand purpose exists on its own yet relates to the company's greater purpose of improving people's lives.

When a brand purpose truly reflects the brand itself, it can take its creative expression in some pretty surprising directions. So, for instance, the underlying truth of Tampax's human brand purpose allowed the famously disciplined P&G to experiment with innovative communications without committing to a wholesale change in direction. Together we created *Zack*, which helped girls learn about their periods in an unusual way: through a series of reality-style online films and stories that tell the tale of 16-year-old Zack Johnson, the first boy to ever experience a period.

Communicating with girls about their period was also the goal of beinggirl.com, which extended P&G's relationship with girls by giving them an online space in which to communicate with one another, ask questions, express themselves, and come to embrace – at their own speed – their periods.

By recognizing that each of its brands has its own purpose for existing, P&G allows its brands to build on their own, authentic personalities to become the ultimate people's brands.

Sept 09, 2003 5:52 PM

Should I tell my friend that guys like

her for the wrong reason?

SunshineGirl

Sept 13, 2003 2:37 PM

Can baking soda and lemon juice

get rid of a hickey?

Jenny_C

FASHION
ALWAYS
RETURNS

TAKE CARE
OF YOUR
CLOTHES

dreft
Laundry
Detergent

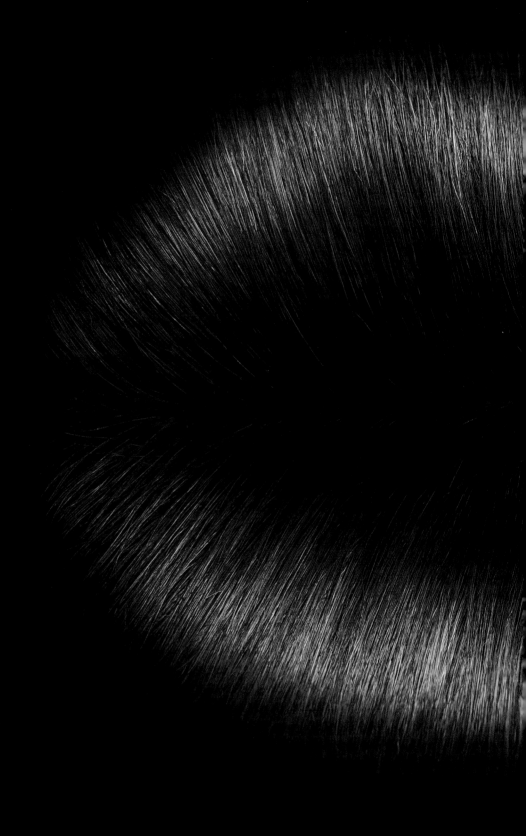

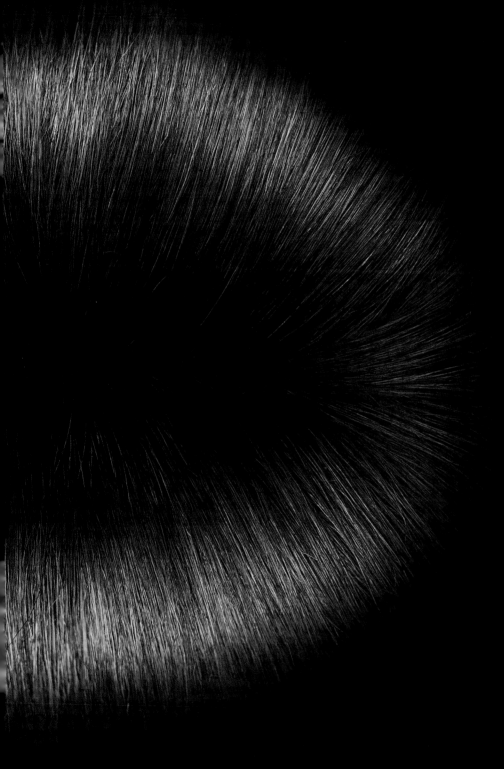

KOLESTON
HAIR COLOURS.
The other you.

ZACK

That boys figure into girls' feelings about their period was an insight that inspired a new way of thinking about how girls relate to this change in their lives. Because *Zack* is so firmly rooted in this human insight, it gave Tampax the opportunity to connect with girls in a way that not only entertained them, but empowered them.

Yubari City Project No Money But Love

When Yubari City, a small town of 12,000 people in the north of Japan known for its Yubari melon and closed coal mines, found itself more than $330 million in debt, it turned to Leo Burnett to help reinvent its reputation and spark financial renewal. Though the town was falling apart, we learned that even under these difficult circumstances, love was keeping people together – Yubari was one of the cities in Japan with the lowest divorce rates. We took this insight into the people of Yubari and helped its officials reinvent their town as the nation's city of love, complete with an official Department of Happy Couples that issued happy-couple certificates. To bring the idea to life (and to attract media attention), we created the Yubari-Fusai, lovable characters whose names played off a linguistic anomaly – "fusai" means both "debt" and "married couple" – to use online and in all the city's communications. In a country obsessed with cute characters like Hello Kitty, the Yubari-Fusai mascot attracted lovebirds from all over Japan who flocked to Yubari, revitalizing the once-downtrodden city as a love-drenched tourist destination.

Subaru Crowd Rider

Subaru's reputation as a manufacturer of stellar cars is as solid as Ayers Rock in Australia's Northern Territory. So when the Leo Burnett team in Sydney was asked by Subaru to help the brand transition from being a trusted one based on the vehicles' function to a coveted one based on its emotional resonance, we knew we'd have to inject some soul into the brand communications (we believed the brand itself was already pretty soulful).

Given what we knew, of Subaru drivers and of likely Subaru drivers, it was clear that from a HumanKind perspective Subaru exists to surround people with support that would, in turn, make them feel confident in their choice of car and in the entire Subaru experience.

To launch its "All 4 The Driver" brand campaign, the team got literal but in a conceptual sort of way. We'll explain: Instead of showing the actual features and functions of the car so people could literally see the technology that was the vehicles' underlying support, the team instead chose to think about support from a more conceptual,

human lens. Sure, Subaru's symmetrical all-wheel drive is great, both in the outback and in town, but it's the people of Subaru who are the real support behind the brand because the brand is nothing without them. So its *Crowd Rider* television spot shows the people – and not the car, not even for a second – as the real drivers and supporters of the brand.

With an original score performed by the internationally acclaimed College Choir and shot in the scenic streets of Kiev and country roads of Crimea, the spot shows the people of Subaru supporting – literally supporting, with their hands – Subaru drivers as they confidently zip through a variety of conditions that make Subaru's all-wheel drive such an asset. In a pitch-perfect example of "show don't tell," the spot shows people that Subaru, despite all the metal and technology and design savvy, is about people, and people are safe in Subaru's hands. And that safety is something to covet.

Crowd Rider conveys a powerful visual message about Subaru's personality as a company. Rather than detailing all the innovative technology in its vehicles, Subaru chose instead to focus on the ways in which that technology serves those who purchase Subarus by showcasing the people behind the brand as drivers cruise through city and country roads.

Purpose

Purpose shifts the conversation from what a product does to what it means

For brands to make real, human connections, we need to put a human purpose at their center. A brand without a purpose will never be understood or embraced.

A human brand purpose is simply a concise articulation of why a brand exists, what it believes, and what it's trying to do.

A human brand purpose is bigger than any brand promise, bigger than any brand position, bigger than any brand proposition, and bigger than any brand function.

A human brand purpose is not about what a brand does or how it does it, but *why* it does it.

Purpose tells us what a brand believes and what it's going to do about it.

Purpose tells us how and where and why and when a brand fits into a person's life – and the value it provides.

Human brand purposes resonate with audiences instantly because they're true and authentic. (If they don't resonate instantly, they need to be rethought.) Notice the word "authentic." That's key – a brand's human purpose must be true to everything about the brand.

Authentic purpose creates an experience that encourages equally authentic conversation. It shifts the conversation from what a product does to what it means. From buying a Hallmark card to send to your mother on Mother's Day to buying a Hallmark card to deepen the relationship with a person you love.

From proposition to purpose.

The beauty of discovering a brand's human purpose is that it propels all manner of marketing activity. The purpose is the power behind the communications, driving the brand forward to achieve something important.

That brands should be governed by convictions and have purpose isn't a new concept (though it's still shockingly underutilized). What *is* powerful and new is the idea that a purpose can replace pretty much everything else in the marketing protocol. A lot of people may talk about purpose, but if you apply it to brand thinking in a creative and dramatic and real way it becomes the *central motivating force* of the brand.

In other words, it's not just another way of describing a brand strategy, it's a way of judging and generating everything a brand does, says, asks, offers, and delivers.

It makes sense to say that Norton from Symantec exists to keep your computer free from online threats and malicious software.

But imagine the inspiring effect of saying: *Norton exists because it believes digital freedom is an inalienable right.* Think about the possibilities this opens up that neither the proposition nor function alone do not.

It makes sense to say that Allstate exists to make sure you get reimbursed quickly if you are in a car accident or your house is robbed.

But imagine the inspiring effect of saying: *Allstate exists because it believes people should live their lives free from fear every day, not just some day.*

It makes sense for DeVry University, which has campuses across the United States and in Canada, to say that it provides an education that will help you get a job.

IN THE HANDS OF A CYBERCRIMINAL, A COMPUTER IS A WEAPON.
EVERY CLICK MATTERS.

Norton from symantec

But imagine the inspiring effect of saying: *DeVry exists because it believes in the value of a practical education, not an ornamental one.*

A human brand purpose plays a practical role as much as it does a directive, conceptual and inspirational one. It can redirect how and where a brand spends money, it can open a brand's eyes to new audiences, it can trigger brand improvements and extensions. It can remind a brand (and those who buy it, as well as those who work for it) why it exists and why it's still needed, desired, and sometimes coveted.

Brands that have a purpose have conviction and a compulsion to change things, to have a role in the world. They try to close the gap between the way the world is and how they wish it were. They are change agents, experience innovators driven to do lots of things to achieve their goals. That's how they draw – and exert – their energy.

That said, it's true that some brands that lack a brand purpose thrive for a while. They produce work that speaks directly to our emotions. Or they produce work that's startlingly – and momentarily – original.

But work that speaks only to our emotions pulls the heartstrings of the lowest common emotional denominator.

It's sentimental and transient.

Creative output like this may move people emotionally but it won't move them to change their behavior.

Likewise, work grounded only in originality is egotistical and ephemeral. It may get people's attention but it won't trigger a behavior change.

In neither case is there long-term benefit.

And that's why brands that do not have convictions and an authentic brand purpose do not, in the end, have powerful, enduring creative engines. Their identity and energy are external – applied or assigned but not true. Eventually their energy sputters and so too do those brands.

Unlike a proposition or an objective, a brand purpose can never be fully achieved or exhausted because by its very nature, "purpose" is ongoing. It has neither a beginning nor an end. Purpose encourages a series of connected achievements but doesn't provide for conclusion. That's why work driven by a human brand purpose, and grounded in the sweet spot where humanity and originality meet, is self-sustaining, compelling, and different.

In its elemental truth, a human brand purpose is the beginning of creating a lifelong relationship with people. It drives creativity that provides opportunity for humans to do something – to participate in ways that speak to their behavior and needs.

A human brand purpose is the engine that drives creative output and the yardstick by which that output is judged.

A human brand purpose is a springboard for creativity that both changes human behavior and unifies broad populations around a brand.

A human brand purpose is what rallies people and creates brand populism.

Think about Nike, a brand with a purpose much deeper than simply offering sporting gear. Nike is about enabling the athlete in each of us, helping everyone strive to perform his or her best. With a clearly defined purpose like this, it's no surprise the creative work that follows is some of the best in its class. The Nike+ effort is a perfect example, an electronic link between shoes, Apple iTunes, and a unique computer application that measures runners' individual progress, tracks goals, and even allows users to challenge their peers.

Or consider Starbucks, a company that doesn't simply sell coffee, but delivers an experience by becoming a familiar, daily refuge for people all around the world.

Or T-Mobile, a telecom brand that understands its core purpose is to facilitate sharing, thus its tagline "Life's for sharing." It's a purpose that's been actualized through flashmob events like a three-minute spontaneous dance routine in a London train station that captivated passersby, inspiring them to film the joyful event on their mobile phones and share the moment with friends. The film went on to become one of the most successful viral campaigns of all time.

Discovering Purpose

It's one thing to say a brand needs a human brand purpose in order to have a reason to exist, maintain relevance, and build a future. It's another thing to identify what that purpose is. To be real, to be authentic, you can't apply a purpose to a brand. Nor can you choose a purpose because you like the way it sounds. The purpose lurks within. It already exists. It's just waiting to be unearthed.

We've devised a framework that allows us to discover a brand's authentic purpose – a "framework," not a codified process, because we don't want to limit what we can do, where we can go, and how we can get there. After all, every brand is different, as are its needs, history, context, and the personalities of the people who work on it, whether they're in manufacturing, communications, logistics, or management. Cultures and customs are different around the globe, too, and those differences must be taken into account when identifying purpose and how it will benefit people.

To apply a cookie-cutter process to identifying purpose would defeat the purpose (pun intended). If we don't allow for tangents, deviations, and digressions we're inhibiting creativity, thought, and ultimately, results.

But it is just that: a framework – with guidance, suggestions, and a roadmap included. It is intended to spark discussion, inspire observation, motivate thinking, stir emotions, arouse pioneering thinking, and trigger connections between disparate ideas, points of view, positions, opinions, and systems.

We call this framework a Purpose Workshop and we've used it around the world to great effect. It's centered around a series of "investigations" that help us understand who we are trying to reach, the behavior we are trying to achieve, the cultural fuel – *the zeitgeist* – influencing society, the conviction that grounds and defines a brand, and finally, a brand's purpose.

Intense, daylong (and in some cases, days-long) events, Purpose Workshops are not secret, behind-closed-doors meetings so the agency can turn around and make a big, dramatic *voila*-worthy reveal at the end to show the client how brilliant it is. Instead, Purpose Workshops include people who occupy corner offices and people who sit in cubicles, people from every area of the agency who work on the account, as well as from partner agencies and, importantly, from the brand itself. Purpose Workshops are open and transparent to take into account the widest possible variety of perspectives, opinions, ideas, talents, and backgrounds.

No two Purpose Workshops are the same since no two brands are the same. Workshops include a wide variety of exercises, tools, discussion topics, and pre-workshop assignments and post-workshop follow-up that identify where people's tensions, anxieties, needs, and aspirations intersect with your brand and its category.

What Purpose Workshops share, however, is a result – a human brand purpose – that is true to what the brand has always been, what the brand is at that very moment, and where that brand wants to go in the future.

who

behavior

cultural
fuel

conviction

purpose

A series of "investigations" creates a Purpose Workshop

Each "investigation" yields brand-specific questions

What are they doing more of? Less of?

What is ok to do today that wasn't yesterday?

How have people changed their social behavior?

How do people behave differently at home? at work? on vacation?

How have people changed how they move, communicate, travel, commute?

In what ways have people's eating, drinking, and grooming and beauty habits changed?

How have people changed their behavior when using technology?

How have people changed their health behavior?

What's new – texting? – that people are doing? What's old – land lines? – and disappearing?

Do people use the product differently?

Why?

Who

Who is the brand trying to reach?

Who has it reached in the past? Are some of those people no longer within reach?

Who does it want to connect with in the future?

Does it want to continue talking to the same people?

Why?

Behavior

How have people changed their purchasing behavior?

What have they stopped or started doing?

Cultural fuel

What tensions in attitudes or behavior exist between rural and urban? early adopters, mainstream, and late adopters? generations? men and women? wealthy and poor?

What major events – natural disasters, economic crashes, terrorist attacks, protests, coups, food shortages – are affecting society?

How have society's values changed?

How has the workplace changed?

What are the top 10 issues on the minds of the people in your region?

What is the media paying the most attention to?

How would you describe the lives of people in your country to someone who has never been there?

What do people miss from their past and want to regain?

Are there new groups in society that weren't there before?

What's happening in society that's threatening your brand or your category?

Why?

Conviction

What are all the things that are true and enduring about the brand?

How has the brand's mission changed from the founder's vision?

What does the brand do for people?

What beliefs does this reflect?

What made the brand so successful?

What do the brand's fans say about it?

What makes people who work on the brand excited?

If the brand disappeared, who would care?

What would be missed?

What events, causes, or other things does it support that help explain its beliefs?

How does the brand behave when times are bad?

Does it stick by its values?

What are the things that the brand never gives up on or never compromises?

What long-standing beliefs or behaviors no longer work for the brand and should be eliminated?

If new management came to the company, what would be held "sacred" and never touched?

Why?

Purpose

What business is the brand really in?

What role does the brand play in people's lives? What does it *do* for people?

What is the higher-order benefit the brand fulfills?

What are people really searching for?

What unfulfilled needs do people have that this brand could fulfill?

What hopes and dreams does the brand encourage?

What fear and anxiety does the brand remove?

What does the brand help you to cope with or what pressure does it relieve?

What does the brand liberate you from or free you to do?

What does the brand encourage or challenge?

What does the brand inspire you to think and feel and do?

Is there any outlet of expression that the brand provides?

Is there anything the brand helps make possible?

Why?

Shelter House of Cards

The best HumanKind work not only identifies a human brand purpose and uses that purpose to inspire and execute extraordinary HumanKind work, but it actually broadens the possibilities for all brands within that category to communicate with people in ways that speak to how we live today; how we think; and what we covet, enjoy, despair, fear, or love. Sometimes this category-*redefining* moment is for a profit-driven brand, but it's no less powerful when it's for a nonprofit brand less worried about controlling a market than it is about helping people better control their lives.

Shelter, a UK-based housing and homelessness charity, has at its core a pretty clear functional purpose – to help people without housing get some and to help people not lose the houses they already have. But its HumanKind purpose is much bigger. Housing – a roof over one's head, a warm bed in which to sleep and dream, a table to share meals with family – goes to the heart of human dignity. Without a house to live in that's safe and clean and not under constant threat of foreclosure, for instance, it is hard if not impossible to feel completely valued as a human.

But charities like Shelter can no longer depend on creating awareness and change merely by showing images of people in misery and pain. To break through to a public often fatigued with the needs of others, in 2008 Shelter literally changed the rules of public service and charity communications with its integrated Shelter "House of Cards" campaign, rooted in the human insight that today – especially today – when the global economy can collapse in just a few news cycles and take down millions of people along with it, it's no longer just the poor

and perennially needy who often need help, but the everyday man and woman who may have previously thought themselves secure from the housing crisis. One false step, one fierce wind, and a lifetime of work and hope can all come crashing down. This brilliant human insight totally resonated with the British public. Anyone can lose their home.

In fact, as Shelter made clear, in many ways we are all living in a "House of Cards," a metaphor that everyone can relate to because it's based in an anxiety rooted deep in the human psyche. It's no longer about the other; today the other is you.

To communicate this insight and make people aware that Shelter can help (and itself needs help), Leo Burnett in the UK took the concept of a house of cards and made it real through a 60-second *House of Cards* television spot that featured an unforgettable landscape dense with emotional there-but-for-the-grace-of-God-go-I power – yet without talking heads or trite, sad-sack imagery. *House of Cards* spoke stirringly to the real-life struggles and uncertainties shared by so many. The spot's spectacular visual effects were amplified through an inspired choice of music by the band Radiohead (the first time the band had allowed its music to be used commercially in the UK). Posters, direct mail, and a Web site were all a part of the campaign.

HOUSE OF CARDS

This incredibly detailed spot shows everyday brick-and-mortar residential buildings instantaneously transforming into flimsy structures made from playing cards as a haunting soundtrack plays, giving Londoners a powerful reminder of how fleeting stability and security had been for so many people during the UK housing crisis.

scarabeus cornuplura

8 8

8 8

To bring the "House of Cards" concept to life even more, the campaign also included an actual house of cards set among thousands of tents at the world-famous Glastonbury music festival and an exhibition in which Shelter commissioned some of the United Kingdom's most creative minds – including artists and designers like Damien Hirst, David Bailey, Vivienne Westwood, Nick Parks, Sir Terence Conran, Neville Brody, and the late Alexander McQueen – to create a unique deck of cards. Each artist-generated card was subsequently exhibited at the Haunch of Venison Gallery in Piccadilly, London, and auctioned off to the highest bidders. (Also available were limited edition decks of replica cards.)

A variety of other HumanKind touches were a part of the lead-up to the exhibit and auction, including a competition in which people everywhere were invited to submit designs for the eight of clubs, with the winner voted on by the public online. Almost 340,000 people voted for a winning design, which was included in the exhibit and limited-edition deck.

The Shelter "House of Cards" campaign spoke to something innate in people and broadened awareness of a situation in the UK to which many thought themselves immune.

7 SHELTER

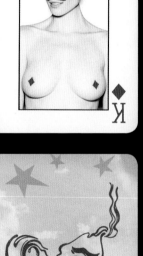

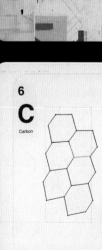

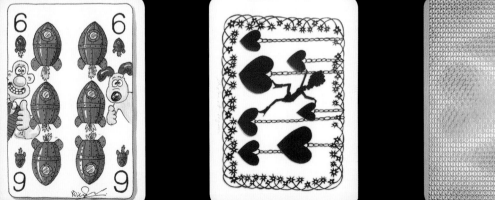

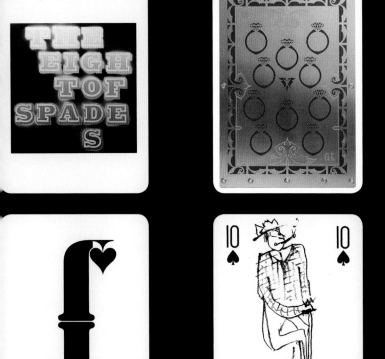

Coca-Cola First Coke of the Year

China's 1.3 billion people share a deep and abiding connection to the Chinese New Year, a time of redemption, forgiveness, compassion, and community. We knew, however, that China's youth yearns to refresh old rituals, to make them more relevant, more contemporary. Given this insight, Coke in China sought to create a meaningful and purposeful role for the brand during the New Year by providing China's people with a modern, new, annual tradition they could call their own – one that would reflect their lives today, invite their participation, and give them a meaningful, creative way to connect with other people and express themselves. And, importantly, one that they would forever associate with Coca-Cola, already the number-one-selling cola in China.

Since the Chinese New Year was also a time in which family and friends shared time together, then why not take the act of sharing the first Coke of the year and turn it into a symbol of optimism and goodwill for the year ahead? To kick-off the first "First Coke of the Year" we knew Coke would have to create a mythology around the idea, to communicate its meaning and possibilities for sharing and for deepening important relationships.

No story of redemption, hope, and optimism looms larger in the Chinese public eye than that of the great athlete Liu Xiang, whose Achilles heal forced him to limp off the track during the 2008 summer Olympics in Shanghai, kiboshing the hope of the nation while the world watched. Working with him, Coke created a 45-second film during which his real-life father consoles Liu Xiang and gives him his first Coke of the year, which symbolized the nation's forgiveness and

ability to understand and move forward from the disappointment. Shown on television, online, and even on taxi seatback LEDs, the film resonated positively with the Chinese people and asked them who *they* would share their first Coke of the year with.

This restored sense of national pride deepened further when Chinese basketball legend Yao Ming was shown on the Chinese New Year visiting Liu Xiang during his recovery to also share his first Coke of the year, offering the Chinese people another collective opportunity to reflect on their hopes for the upcoming year.

Everyday people were invited to share not only their first Coke of the year with those they love, but also their feelings about the experience, online at icoke.cn – and did they ever! The site registered more than 72 million page views; almost 5.2 million homemade videos, animated films, photos, and stories were posted there and on other social media sites; and more than 21 million e-cards were sent. A massive New Year's celebration party in Beijing, complete with music, dancing, and celebrities in attendance sharing their first Coke of the year, cemented this new New Year's ritual in the minds of the Chinese people.

By giving the Chinese people a voice and an opportunity to participate, Coke transformed them from observers of the brand to achievers *with* the brand – the goal of HumanKind – and itself came to embody a new tradition.

你想与谁分享?

Coca-Cola, one of China's most loved brands has become synonymous with uplifting refreshment

Red Cross The Store That Sells Hope

Guilt, as a way to connect with people emotionally, is losing its *oomph.* Hope on the other hand, has real possibilities. At least, that's what our team in Lisbon hoped when the Red Cross there asked Leo Burnett to help it raise money during the Christmas holidays. So instead of turning to the typical guilt-centric holiday "ask" most nonprofit organizations fall back on, we stepped back, sat down, closed our eyes, and asked ourselves (and our client) what the human brand purpose of the Red Cross is beyond the functional – food for the hungry, blankets for the weary, water for the parched, and first aid for the sick. Why, beyond these and many other important activities, does the Red Cross exist? It exists to give hope; it's purpose is to give hope.

Hope is what it sells. Hope is its product. Hope is the merch.

But if hope is all that – something, in other words, people could neither hear, taste, touch, see, wear, use, display, read, flaunt, or gift wrap – where would we sell it? In a store, of course, like most other things for sale. So we rented a storefront in Galerias Monumental, one of Lisbon's busiest shopping malls, and designed a sleek, modern boutique both like and unlike any other. Like, because the Red Cross Store+ had shelves, hangers, dressing rooms, display windows, and of course, cash registers and receipts. But unlike, because unlike the more than 100 other stores in the mall jammed with shiny new things, Store+ sold only hope, a shopping experience that gave people the satisfaction of both a traditional mall transaction and the act of giving to those in need.

Like any other store grand opening, in the weeks leading up to it a communications program that included television, radio, banners, billboards, posters, direct marketing, and an online presence blitzed the city. The response was enormous, with hundreds of people lining up on opening night, countrywide media attention, including from all three major television networks, and sales of "hope" so high that on opening day the store was among the top 10 in the entire mall. The store became such a popular shopping destination that it extended its opening hours and closing date.

The Red Cross Store+ was so successful at expressing the human purpose of the brand compellingly and with imagination that the Red Cross in other cities around the world asked for similar retail experiences. Red Cross Store+ opened in Madrid's upscale Xanadú shopping center the following holiday season, with its own unique twist: shelves lined with brightly colored books had titles that implied stories of hope lay between their covers, yet inside those pages were blank, waiting for people to buy hope so those stories of renewal could begin.

While customers left the Red Cross store of hope with empty hands, their hearts were full, a sure sign that the experience not only resonated with them emotionally, but changed the way they see the act of giving.

STORE➕

Visitors to Lisbon's Red Cross Store+
had a shopping experience not unlike
any other, except that hope was the
lone thing for sale.

Homebase Railway Station

Like many railway stations in the United Kingdom, Carlisle Railway Station is a crenellated pile whose interior was, at best, drab. Built in 1847, renovations to its interior décor were few and far between. As a place through which commuters and travelers pass on their way to London 300 miles to the south or Glasgow 100 miles to the north, it lacked a certain…charm. At least, that is, it did until Homebase, the UK's second largest home improvement retailer, gave it a makeover to show people that any everyday space – a railway station, their own houses and flats – could be made into a cheerful, contemporary, and comfortable home.

Droves of workers took over the station, painting walls, hanging wallpaper, placing cozy couches and chairs, rigging up chandeliers, arranging garden furniture, laying flooring and sod, even installing more kitchen units. Most spectacularly of all, the wide bridge over which thousands passed every day was painted in Technicolor stripes. Soon, weary commuters and tired travelers were lounging about, feeling quite at home. Many liked the new look so much they created a Facebook page to encourage the city to make it permanent – in fact, out of a city with just over 100,000 people, almost 10,000 joined the "Keep Carlisle train station like this!" page.

While the setting was used as a backdrop for a television advertisement and garnered media attention throughout the country, the entire endeavor, which also included a makeover contest, invited people to participate in the brand in a new and unique way.

Time
Destination
07:46 LONDON EUSTON
Expected
Calling at:
On Time
Virgin Pendolino
07:4138
DEPARTURES
3

Luxor Writing Instruments Highlight What's Important

Most people look at a highlighter and think it merely does a single thing – highlighting information they need. Our team in Mumbai looked at Luxor Highlighters and saw a dual purpose – an instrument that highlights information people need and, simultaneously, eliminates the information they don't. To bring this bifurcated insight to life, it took a two-pronged approach. First, it chose several well-known historical figures whose faces would be identifiable even in silhouette and it wrote their life stories so that the words filled an entire newspaper page.

He has kept us laughing till we cried and made us cry till we laughed for the better part of the last century. He has been called the most influential actor and artist of his times. But he was much more than that. He was possibly one of the most influential personalities of the 1900's. His work is studied even today in the most sophisticated of film schools and even after that, our generation can not boast of a talent as obvious, or as prolific. His most famous character - the man with the toothbrush mustache, bowler hat, bamboo cane and funny walk, aka, 'The Little Tramp' - won him acclaim, notoriety and the hearts of millions through generations. His personal and professional life is a montage of success and scandal, laughter and pain, adoration and persecution and, at the end of it all, immortality. Born in London on April 16, 1889, Charles Spencer Chaplin, spent his childhood in shabbily furnished rooms, state poorhouses and an orphanage. He was never sure who his real father was; his mother's husband Charles Chaplin, a singer, deserted the family early and died of alcoholism in 1901. His mother, Hannah Harriet Hill, also known as Lily Harvey, a small-time actress, was in and out of mental hospitals through her life and after she retired from the stage, she earned just enough for her two sons and herself through sewing. Charlie and his elder half-brother Sidney were inseparable and as they grew, they became each others closest friends and confidants. It was a relationship that would endure past the fame and its attendant ills. His brother went on to become his agent and continued to be his closest aide till his death in 1965. Sidney left home first, working as a deckhand on board a ship and then later moved to a career on stage. While his younger half-brother, Charlie Chaplin made his stage debut at The Canteen, a theatre at Aldershot Military Town. The theatre was renowned to be one of the worst places to perform for anybody, leave alone for a young child at the tender age of five. His troubled mother was booed off after she failed to sing on stage. The audience pelted her with missiles and reduced her to tears. While his mother was dealing with her reception on the stage and while she cried and argued with her manager backstage, a legend was about to be born. A little boy took hold of his destiny and in a boyish attempt to save his mother further pain and ridicule, the young Charles Chaplin stepped on and sang a well known tune, Jack Jones. The audience was amazed at both the courage of a child that young and the very obvious talent that Charles displayed that night. He won the riotous crowd over and he never really got off that stage. From then - his first night on stage at Aldershot-young Chaplin went on to perform across the British Vaudeville circuit. From those early days on, his extraordinary athleticism, grace, timing and genius, set Chaplin apart. In 1910, at the age of 21, an opportunity presented itself to Chaplin. It was a chance to travel to the new world of entertainment and so he made his first trip to America with Fred Karno's Speechless Comedians. On his first journey across, Charlie realised that his life was about to change forever. He was on his way to new fortune and on his first night in New York's theatre district, Chaplin was dazzled with the bustle and lights. Chaplin claims to have told himself that this was 'it'. "This is where I belong." Yet he never became a US citizen. Charlie Chaplin toured with this troupe for two years and after five months back in England, he returned to the United States, for the second time. He and another youngster, Arthur Stanley Jefferson, aka Stan Laurel arrived in America with the Karno troupe. While with the Karno company, Chaplin came to the attention of more than a few prospective employers. But the eventual credit for really discovering him gets added to the tally of filmmaker Mack Sennet, who hired him for his studio, the Keystone Film Company. This was the window that Chaplin had been looking for. It was just the very opportunity he had come to America for and it was Charlie's first foray into the new and exciting medium of film, but his performance and ideas were hailed and applauded by critics and the audiences alike. This film was his maiden venture, but its runaway success belied that fact. Though *Making a Living*, became a national hit, Chaplin was unhappy with the film on a creative level. Sennet's films all had a certain formula to them and Chaplin was left dismayed with the typical slapstick speed and bathing beauty escapades that were Sennet's speciality. In Sennet's comedies, one notices the obvious celebration of the flexibilities of the medium. Simply revelling in the medium, in Sennet's work, speechlessness raised itself to a racket, but Chaplin understood that visibility needed leisure as a respite. He realised that a lot more could be said that way than through exaggeration. He got the pathos of a look as well as silence, to work its most intimate magic. In all his films Chaplin ensured that the actor (who was the paint, the tool, the word) spoke, through the art of acting. The artist, not the medium talked, so the actor and not the camera did the acting. It was for his next film that Chaplin created his trademark iconic character and introduced him to the public. For *Kid Auto Races At Venice*, Chaplin created the personality of the 'Little Tramp' character. Chaplin had no idea of the character until he put his ensemble together. The jacket was too tight, pants too baggy, the hat too small the boots too big. The Tramp was one whole contradiction. As he put on the now famous costume, the character slowly formed in Chaplin's mind and he was rapidly developing traits and idiosyncrasies as he went along. The smirks, wide eyes, walk and other unique mannerisms were fully born by the time Chaplin walked out to face the camera. The Tramp was funniest when trying to extricate himself from the most difficult and trying situations and when he was most afraid, mincing and smirking as he tried unsuccessfully to placate the outraged. He constantly skidded around corners, teetering dangerously out of control, standing up for those weaker than himself and changing a pat to a shove when most needed. He was the complete underdog, the small man and the real American hero. Chaplin's obvious talent made the astute Mack Sennet hand over complete creative control. Chaplin was soon entrusted with directing and editing his own films and he made 34 shorts for Sennet in his first year. Among these films was also the acclaimed landmark comedy feature, *Tillie's Punctured Romance*. In 1915, Chaplin eventually signed a more favourable contract with Essanay Studios adding new depth to his style. The owners, Spoor and Anderson ('S' and 'A') commissioned Charlie Chaplin to do a number of films. These new and decidedly more involving films were more ambitious and ran twice as long as the Keystone movies. In fact, even years later, both the studios re-cut their Chaplin films and distributed them as new ones. A year of very inventive comedies followed and later, he was paid US$670,000 by the Mutual Film Corporation (a salary that made Charlie Chaplin the highest paid entertainer in the world). Chaplin was paid to shoot, star and exclusively produce as many as a dozen two-reel comedies. Each of the 12 films that Chaplin created were in themselves masterpieces. Chaplin aficionados and fans believe that these films he produced rank among what can easily be called the most influential comedies in history. Practically every Mutual film from this project was a runaway success, and the viewing public and critics worldwide agreed that each comedy was a classic. The much acclaimed *Easy Street, One AM* and *The Adventurer* are perhaps the best known. After the end of the Mutual contract in 1917, Chaplin signed a very lucrative deal with First National to direct and produce eight two-reel comedies. With the new First National deal he started his own Hollywood studio. Although First National expected Chaplin to do short comedies, he expanded them into feature length films. Trust and this total and absolute freedom allowed Chaplin to create timeless classics like *The Kid* (1921). Also included in this initial set of truly endearing films are classics like, *Shoulder Arms* (1918) and *The Pilgrim* (1923). At or approximately about this time, Chaplin co-founded the United Artists film distribution firm which gave him complete control of his film productions and assured him independence. Chaplin founded this company along with friends and a few fellow film artists who were all seeking to escape from the monopoly that bigger studios had in the industry and who were controlling the kinds of films being made. This was a growing practice in Hollywood within the old studio system. Under this banner, Chaplin and his partners quickly compiled a body of work that still endures till this day. With the complete creative control in their hands, these artists created and made a number of new masterpieces. Chaplin resisted the growing trend of making talkies and even when he first did, sound was mainly through musical score and props instead of dialogue. It was the arrival, the total public acceptance and development of sound that Chaplin had to confront and equal in his craft of film making. He believed that actors were much more effective communicating through silence in films. He steadfastly and sincerely considered good cinema to be more involving with the power of silence to aid it - like Chinese symbolism meaning different things as per its scenic connotation. Film was most essentially a truly visual and pantomimic art. In fact, in his interview with Time magazine he dared one to describe a wart hog to a group and then show the picture to realise the difference. In his movie, *City Lights*, Charlie Chaplin honestly displayed this art to the fullest. This movie has been well acclaimed and it's believed to be one of the finest examples of the art form of acting that the medium of film has seen. Of the culminative scene the feted critic Agee said that this was possibly the most poignant part of not just Chaplin's films, but of all cinema of the 20th century. In fact he goes on to state that it was definitely the "greatest single demonstration of any acting committed to celluloid." Although Chaplin himself believes that his *Gold Rush* (1925) was the film he would like to be remembered by, *City Lights* has really endured. Chaplin finally gave in some years later and when he made his first film with sound, the public was eager to see how this master of the silent era would perform. Chaplin's new production was the very controversial talkie, *The Great Dictator* (1940). The new film, an open defiance against a man who had plunged the world into the worst armed conflict ever was a landmark event. The film, a reaction against the corrupt and against Adolf Hitler and Nazism was made just a year before America abandoned its stance of isolationism to enter World War II. This movie brought to the fore the evil of anarchy and it was the perfect film for America just before it entered the war. This bold film was seen as an act that surpassed monetary necessities and actually took a stand. Though Chaplin hated patriotism, he could not stand injustice either. The movie was full of courage considering the political climate of the time. At the conclusion of the film, the two characters Chaplin portrayed, the Jewish barber and the dictator swapped places through a complex plot and eventually at the end of the feature Chaplin addresses the crowds as the dictator 'Adenoid Hynkel'. He launches into a speech to the multitude gathered to hear their leader talk (again identical to the pictures of the rise of Hitler) and the viewers together with a rousing speech. Chaplin put to rest any doubts people might have had of his ability to perform through sound. He began by imploring the public to feel. Urging everyone of us to finally stand up. To hope. To resist. To believe. Chaplin seemed to have picked up the gauntlet with this last monologue, turning it into one of the great speeches of all time. This genius went on to create and make many more dialogue films, but the American public's love of this most famous of comics was on the wane. The publicity surrounding his life caused fans to stay away and it seemed his work was on the decline. Chaplin was vilified by the yellow press and was facing serious criminal and civil charges for his indiscretions. But there was a deeper rage against him along with the problems related to his involvement with actress Joan Barry. In 1947, his black comedy *Monsieur Verdoux* was met with protests in many US cities. But Chaplin stoically made the films he believed in. During the McCarthy era, Chaplin was accused of un-American activities and was a suspected communist. J Edgar Hoover tried repeatedly to end Chaplin's temporary stay, since he had not applied for US residency and he finally achieved that in 1952. Chaplin unwittingly left for the UK for his London premiere of *Limelight* and his re-entry permit was revoked. He is said to have been sadddened by this harassment. Chaplin then decided not to try to come back to the States for good and his family chose to live in Switzerland. Chaplin returned to the United States only in 1972 decades later, after the mood in America had come full circle; to receive an Oscar for his 1952 film, *Limelight* to an emotional welcome and he was given the longest standing ovation in the history of the Oscars. It was a truly poignant moment in modern film history even though this was actually his second Academy Award; his disdain for the first one that was initially awarded to him back in 1929 for his hilarious film *The Circus*, was the reason for the gap; despite making many films far better than *The Circus*. In 1975, this man of humble and modest beginnings was knighted by Queen Elizabeth II. His life, though fraught at the start with troubles that would have crippled most of us, was full. His story, though peppered with scandal and controversy, will always be considered one of the most inspiring stories of our times. Chaplin was undoubtedly a versatile entertainer and has kept us in splits and that was how he connected. He did not restrict himself to being an entertainer, but has instead used his work, like most artists, to comment on the ills that effect our lives. He understood the human condition and realised that he could touch and even help change society. Which explains why, almost a century after he first started out, Chaplin still endures. His plots and his characters, in a larger sense, battle with core human themes, so his work still continues to be relevant. His characters, from the Little Tramp to Adenoid Hynkel, will always address issues pertinent to life, not just the era that they lived in. So he is now immortal and his comments still ring true and the lessons Chaplin so carefully laced his comedies with, will still be relevant a long time from now. The change that Chaplin pursued has been the Holy Grail for thinkers and will continue to be so even a century from now. Mainly because Chaplin believed in content over style and in hope over desperation. He believed that through humour, the pathos of the human situation could best be conveyed and he believed in action over talk. He believed in the good that lies buried deep in the unconscious of the sleeping multitude, despite his treatment by those same people. And he believed that if you really tried, you could touch the heart of humanity and he was hopeful that we could find the ability to do that through film. How far then is Charlie Chaplin from the all too obvious clown? Chaplin gives us a true fortune in truths and we need to, as a people, all tap into it. He dares us to ask him the questions that worry and nag our collective beliefs and we are shocked when this simple little character provides us those very answers. We are incredulous and amazed, "You?" like the Tramp is asked in that famous movie, *City Lights*, by the heroine. As she is finally delivered from blindness we watch as her romantic aspirations slowly die on seeing who her saviour is. While like in *City Lights*, and like the Tramp, Chaplin, too must be figuratively looking at us. His face caught in a tight close up - a map of pride, shame and devotion, as he stares back at us through his honest body of work, as the Tramp did then, he still nods and purses his lips in modesty. Imagine that! The odd little man is a teacher, friend, philosopher and guide, not just to a select few but to the whole of humanity. A shrug and a grimace later, he finally says, "Yes." This is not to say that Chaplin did no[illegible] There were enough critics who considered him to be nothing more than a fairly obvious clown. There are enough moralists who believed his life was a reflection of decadence and [illegible] in an attempt to appear less common call out that 'Buster Keaton was the true great comedian of that time.' But these are not the people Chaplin was ever talking to. [illegible] popularity, coming third in a Charlie Chaplin look-alike contest he entered in for a lark. While all those around him were losing their heads, he kept his. [illegible] never lost the common touch. Chaplin passed away in his sleep on Christmas Day in 1977, aged eighty eight. He was interred in Corsier-Sur-Vevey Cemetery, Vaud, Switzerland. [illegible] len by a small group of Polish and Bulgarian mechanics in an attempt to extort money from his family. The plot failed, the robbers were captured, and the corpse was recovered eleven weeks later near [illegible] His body was reburied under two metres of concrete to prevent further attempts. But Chaplin's legacy can never really pass. His influence has been continuous and consistent. Filmmaker Mack Sennet thought him to be "just the greatest artist who ever lived." Hart Crane, who wrote a poem about Chaplin, said his pantomime "represents the futile gesture of the poet today." Even the Beat Generation claim to have been inspired by Chaplin, and it is said that Jack Kerouac went on the road because he too wanted to be a hobo. Recently, IBM used the Tramp as the logo to advertise its venture into computers. Chaplin, even today is still selling. Now he is selling dreams. Silently.

The story was written in a very precise manner such that, second, when just the important parts were highlighted – parts that in themselves told a complete, though shorter, version of that person's biography – the face of the subject appeared. Posters of these pages were also displayed on college campuses. Students were challenged to highlight the important parts of each life story; when they highlighted the right parts, the subject would emerge.

Department for Transport Anti-Drug Driving

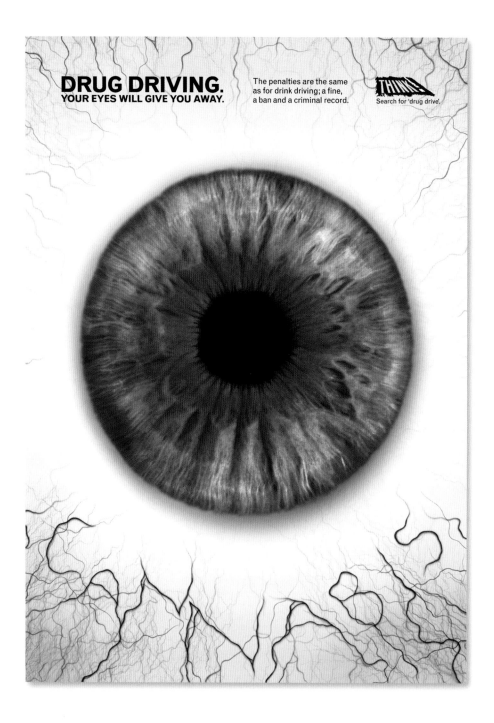

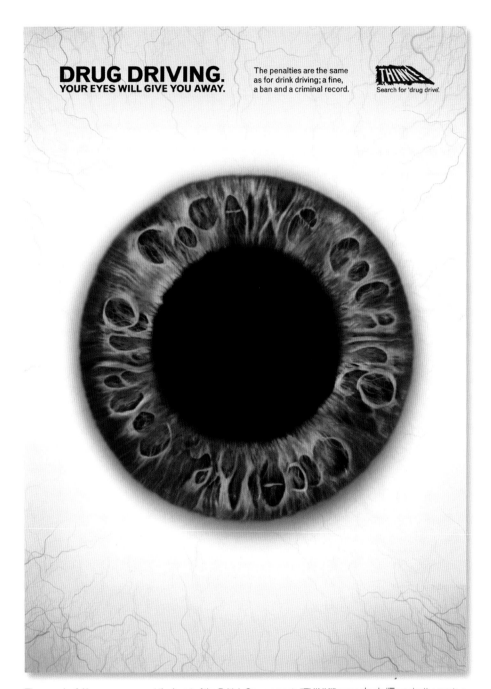

DRUG DRIVING.
YOUR EYES WILL GIVE YOU AWAY.

The penalties are the same as for drink driving; a fine, a ban and a criminal record.

THINK!
Search for 'drug drive'.

The meaningful human purpose at the heart of the British Governments "THINK!" campaign is "To make the roads a safer place." This anti-drug drive campaign on behalf of the government is designed to truly connect with the British people and transform behavior. The penalties are the same as for drunk driving; a fine, a ban, and a criminal record.

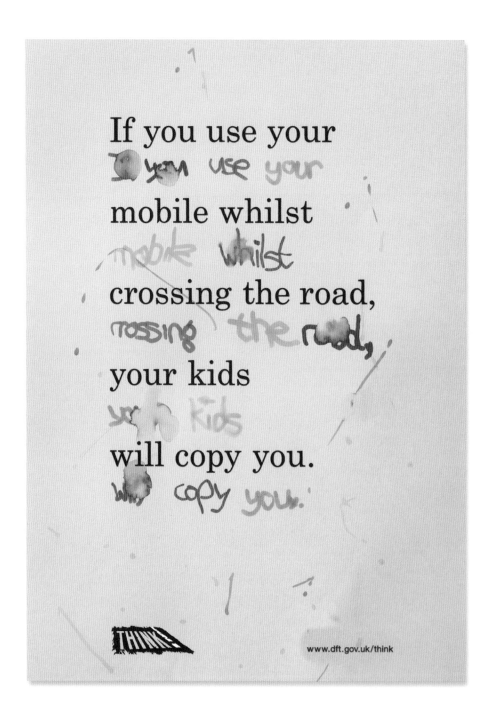

This powerful UK Department for Transport message is rooted in a comprehensive understanding of human behavior and is designed to truly resonate with the British public and make it think twice about road safety.

Allstate Insurance Marina Towers

"You're In Good Hands.®"

It's a simple four-word statement that perfectly captures what Allstate Insurance does, what it means to people, and what its purpose is. In use for over 50 years, it dovetails with our HumanKind approach and allows the company to communicate with people and invite their participation in a huge variety of ways.

The statement – the purpose – is also a stake in the ground that tethers the company's actions to its words. It's why the people at Allstate were instrumental in the development of three-point seat belts and the legislation that made wearing one the law. It's why their research on automotive accident injuries helped lead to the creation of air bags and antilock brakes. It's why they were among the first to warn drivers about the dangers of using cell phones while driving and why they send customers a Safe Driving Bonus® check for driving accident-free.

And it's why they maintain a fleet of Mobile Response Units to quickly get devastated homeowners much-needed assistance after natural disasters.

These acts put people in good hands, whether they're Allstate customers or not.

Allstate's promise to put people in "good hands" has always been backed up by actions like these that give the promise human meaning – actions that allow the promise to take root in an emotional relationship with people that represents much more than a typical relationship between customer and company.

Whether through the parent-teen driving contract, which seeks to protect teenagers with licenses yet little driving experience (more than 50,000 contracts have been downloaded from Allstate's Web site) or something more lighthearted like the television spot in which a car chase through the streets of Chicago ends with a car flying out of a high-rise parking lot and splashing into the Chicago River 17 stories below to showcase the breadth of hazards Allstate addresses, the brand's purpose is always clear.

People count on Allstate because Allstate believes people deserve to feel protected every day, not just some day.

Kellogg's Special K

It's a conceit in popular culture that many women feel if they could only lose that extra five to 10 pounds their lives would be better. The funny thing, however, is that most women don't know what five to 10 pounds looks like. So when Kellogg's Special K cereal gave women the opportunity to lose six pounds in two weeks by taking (and completing) the Special K challenge – replace two meals a day with Special K and lose six pounds in two weeks – we and the brand knew (because we and the brand know women) that we'd have to literally show them what six pounds looks like and would mean to them and their bodies when they lost it.

So through a campaign that ran the gamut of media, Kellogg's invited women into the experience of understanding what six pounds looks and feels like. Among other things, it showed women what a phonebook of weight – coincidentally, a six pounder – looks like (imagine that off your hips); it showed women what six pounds melting off their body (or a snowman's roly-poly body) would look like; it showed women what would happen if they dropped a jeans size (their jeans wouldn't stay up). It showed women, ultimately, that six pounds was worth fighting for – or fighting off, simply by curtailing snacks and substituting two meals a day with a satisfying bowl of Special K.

As the campaign evolved, the team continued to apply the idea that Special K exists to "inspire women to shine," to give women what they need and want, to showcase that it understands women and their attitude toward their weight and how it makes them look and feel. We identified women – real women – and through a variety of media, including television, print, and on a specially designed Web site and a vibrant Facebook page, followed them as they worked toward their goals. It was about their weight loss but even more about what losing that weight would mean to them. "To look in the mirror and like the woman looking back at me…. to hear those four little words, 'have you lost weight?'… My victory? Not using my arms to hide my stomach any more."

The two-week "Special K Challenge" campaign has allowed Special K to avoid the trap of becoming thought of as a "diet food"; instead it has become a vibrant and powerful partner with women, helping them to help themselves look and feel wonderful. It's taken its purpose seriously. Special K isn't about losing weight. It's not about six pounds. It's not even about jeans in a pile at your ankles. It's about inspiring women to shine, which is exactly what the campaign has done for millions of women.

THE GIRL FROM IPANEMA

the girl from Ipanema

lives in Cleveland

A beautiful woman walks along the beach as the surf laps at her feet. Inside every woman lives this sexy, confident "Girl from Ipanema," and Special K will help women find her.

lives in Baltimore

lives in Sacramento

lives in every woman

lure her back out

Special
K

123456789

10111213 14

Eat two bowls a day for two weeks and lose 6 lbs.

Participation

Participation ideas demand a different role for advertising

An act that invites participation is a new unit of marketing that replaces the old unit of marketing, which was an ad. A symbolic language switch perhaps, but an important one nonetheless. It gives us and the brands we represent permission to think about and talk about and create advertising that goes far beyond the traditional. To reconceive advertising's releationship with people we had to start using words that more dynamically and accurately describe the type of advertising we believe in.

Let's face it: messaging as we know it is on life support. Even the word messaging – the result of turning a perfectly serviceable noun into the verb it was never meant to be – reflects its shallowness, inauthenticity, and transience.

Messaging as it's been used by marketers fails to connect with people because it's usually a product of group think emanating from a windowless conference room in a bland office tower in downtown wherever, cut off from life and, worse, cut off from the brand it purportedly represents. That's why so much of today's advertising is so forgettable: It begins with messaging that not only has no relation to people's lives, needs, or dreams, but also no relation to the brand itself.

HumanKind, however, says let's think about messaging later – if we think about it at all. Let's instead start with people, move to purpose, and let everything flow naturally from *there*.

Purpose, after all, gives us the springboard to go in myriad directions, to move beyond passivity to participation, the third key element of HumanKind.

Participation as a consequence of a brand's human purpose is a new way of looking at how brands communicate because acts that allow people to participate feel – and are – authentic. They resonate viscerally. They add to people's lives and they make sense.

Participation moves advertising from ads as propositions, promises, and messages, to acts that involve, invite, delight, challenge, serve, inspire, teach, protect, tempt, and, ultimately, incite behavior change. After all, it's behavior and experience that shape people's attitudes, not vice versa.

Therefore: acts not ads.

When the Grigore Antipa Natural History Museum in Bucharest organized one of the biggest dinosaur exhibitions in the world, bringing skeletons in from as far away as South America, it could have relied on a typical newspaper ad campaign to encourage people to come to the museum. Instead, the museum created a citywide phenomenon that galvanized thousands of people and attracted the media like no standard advertising campaign would have done. After having artists create an exact, life-size replica of a T Rex, it worked with city officials and teachers to bury the "bones" in neighborhood playgrounds and gardens, wherever kids were most likely to be.

Acts n

ot Ads

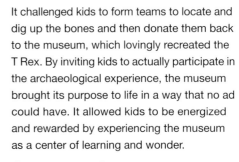

It challenged kids to form teams to locate and dig up the bones and then donate them back to the museum, which lovingly recreated the T Rex. By inviting kids to actually participate in the archaeological experience, the museum brought its purpose to life in a way that no ad could have. It allowed kids to be energized and rewarded by experiencing the museum as a center of learning and wonder.

Acts not ads.

Brazil faced a problem when it cracked down on illegal, electronic, casino-style jackpot machines: What to do with the huge stash of seized machines? With the help of Leo Burnett in Rio de Janeiro, Brasil Telecom stepped in. It turned out that the gambling machines actually housed a powerful 2.3 GHz processor with 30 MB RAM memory – a perfectly functional PC. Brasil Telecom changed the layout a bit, added a keyboard where the drink holder had been, and donated the retrofitted and newly branded Internet-capable machines to local public schools. Kids now had a new learning tool and Brasil Telecom budding relationships with the kids themselves – the company's next generation of customers – as well as the adults in these children's lives.

Acts not ads.

Acts can be extraordinary and beautiful pieces of art that have such emotional, persuasive resonance that they're able to change how people think, like the compelling short film called *Funeral*, created by Leo Burnett in Singapore for the Ministry of Community Development, Youth and Sports, the human purpose of which, despite its name, is to "celebrate families." Turns out that the number of people marrying each year in Singapore is falling, a worrying trend in a country that isn't too populous to begin with. Research indicated it's not that people didn't want to fall in love and marry, but that they were waiting for the impossible: the "perfect" person (you know, someone as financially successful as they were attractive, as generous as they were intelligent, and on and on).

This quietly startling film, which simply depicts a woman delivering a eulogy at her husband's funeral, uses vivid, natural language and a deeply affecting performance to speak to larger issues of love, marriage, and family. It is intended to help people fall in love. After a charming anecdote about her husband's snoring, she says, "Towards the end of his life, when his illness was at its worse, these sounds indicated to me that my David was still alive. And what I wouldn't give just to hear those sounds again before I sleep. In the end, it is the small things that you remember, the little imperfections that make them perfect for you. So, to my beautiful children, I hope one day you too find yourselves life partners who are as beautifully imperfect as your father was for me." The emotional connection she creates with her audience, both among those in the film and by its viewers, is as powerful an act as any. The "Beautifully Imperfect" communications campaign that followed cut across film, public relations, and social media, showcasing how love, in its truest form, is when two people find beauty in their partners imperfections.

An act is anything that constitutes a deed that shows you where the heart of that brand, company, or organization is, what it cares about, what it believes in, and what its *purpose* is. Allstate's teen driving contract, the Red Cross' Store for Hope, Canon's photochain, Kronenbourg beer's can-camera, Fundacion Altius' "Message in a Bottle." If you knew nothing else about these brands yet experienced them through these acts, you would know a lot.

An act is anything that is of substance to people – a gesture, an idea, or an actual thing you touch and play with.

An act is anything that creates emotional connections that deepen over time.

And yes, an act can include ads because ads born from a brand's human purpose can create emotional bonds between people and brands. And that, in and of itself, is an act.

An act does not have to be big; sometimes the smallest are the most powerful. An act does not have to be charitable; creating an act that gives a person a quiet moment of joy can be a great gift. An act can support for-profit companies and nonprofit organizations. An act can contribute to society at large or to a single life.

Purpose-driven acts aren't just clever ideas but, instead, drivers of experiences that play a role in both a person's life *and* in the life of a brand.

It's not unusual for us to think of a wide variety of acts that circle back to a brand's purpose, yet that doesn't mean they are all equally good. Acts must not only reflect the brand's human purpose, but they also must provoke an emotional response; be simple, inclusive and accessible; and relevant to people's lives. They must feel natural, not like a gimmick or stunt.

Consider the Nike Chalkbot, a device launched at the 2009 Tour de France. It's common at the annual race for fans to write words of encouragement with chalk alongside the road. And since millions of cycling enthusiasts can't make the trek, Nike – with the help of some experts – developed a robotic chalking mechanism that was able to receive and process messages from fans via Twitter, SMS codes, or a special Web site. The messages were all photographed and sent back to participants with GPS coordinates of where they were placed. Over the course of the race, the Chalkbot put down more than 100,000 messages in bright, Lance Armstrong LIVESTRONG yellow.

When British rockers Oasis were about to release their album, *Dig Out Your Soul*, they avoided traditional promotion and opted to bring the record directly to the people in advance. The band turned to New York City street performers, teaching them the songs from the record, which they would go on and debut on the streets of the Big Apple. The band posted maps online indicating the performances' locations and the campaign turned into a challenge for Oasis fans to navigate the city for an early urban listening party, weaving itself into the fabric of the city's vibrant music scene at the same time.

In the UK, the chip brand Walkers was looking for a new flavor, so it brought people directly into the effort. With "Do Us A Flavor," it offered 50,000 pounds and a one percent share of future sales to the winner. The idea brought in more than 1.2 million suggestions, literally giving people the opportunity to co-create its brand.

Perhaps the ultimate example of participation in recent years was Barack Obama's 2008 presidential campaign. The effort harnessed the influence of the netroots to connect and empower volunteers. Outreach via Twitter, text messaging, and MyBarackObama.com, a social networking site through which people could establish their own individual profiles, made the election the most participatory of all time.

Acts matter because they lead to the most important part of the equation, HumanKind's fourth element: what we call populism.

Through genuine acts a brand is woven into the social fabric of broad populations in such a way that it becomes a part of the culture. Once this level of success is reached, the success itself becomes self-perpetuating.

It's the *people* who continue to build the brand through their participation with, and involvement in, it.

In the end, advertising agencies do not create iconic brands, people do.

Creating Acts

The truth is, brilliant HumanKind acts can come from anywhere at any time. The key, what all brilliant acts share, is their connection to, and reflection of, a brand's human purpose.

When brainstorming acts we think about the human-brand experience across all touchpoints. What is the overall barrier, struggle, or improvement to a good experience that the brand can deliver against? Can the brand enhance moments of happiness? Can it create excitement or passion where there is apathy? How can the brand create a different kind of experience for people in these moments?

By exploring questions like these we identify where a person's experience with a brand doesn't match up to the brand's human purpose. This disconnect is an important moment of tension. For an act to be successful, it must exist at, illuminate, and exploit that tension.

Isolating and identifying these tension points allow us to write brand act statements specific to our brand.

I seek to create acts of_____ in moments of_____

The first blank connects to the brand's human purpose and the second blank to the human dynamic the brand is responding to. In other words, what is the emotional state that people are experiencing that the brand needs to address? In essence, this identifies a solution (first blank) to a problem (second blank).

A wide variety of emotions can trigger countless necessary tensions

AcceptanceAffectionAlertness
AngerAnnoyanceAnticipationApathy
AppreciationAnxietyAttentiveness
AweBewildermentBetrayalBoredom
CelebrationCompassionConfusion
ConscienceContemptCuriosity
DelightDepressionDesireDisgust
DisappointmentDistressDoubt
EaseEcstasyEmpathyEnmityEnvy
EmbarrassmentEuphoriaFamiliarity
FrightFrustrationFunGenerosity
GratitudeGriefGuiltHappinessHatred
HopeHostilityInterestJealousyJoy
KindnessLongingLoveLustMalice
ModestyNeglectOptimismPatience
PleasurePrideQuietRageRelief
RegretRelaxationRespectRemorse
ResentmentRevengeSadnessShame
StressSufferingSurvivalTogetherness
TruthTimidityUpliftValueWitWonder
XenophobiaYearningZealousness

I seek to create acts of _____
in moments of _____

confidence in moments of doubt	**inspiration** in moments of weakness	**coolness** in moments of social risk
encouragement in moments of insecurity	**progress** in moments of stagnation	**liberation** in moments of constraint
realization in moments of inspiration	**support** in moments of exploration	**togetherness** in moments of loneliness
altruism in moments of selfishness	**refreshment** in moments of stress	**friendship** in moments of indifference
connection in moments of isolation	**casualness** in moments of seriousness	**interest** in moments of timidity
sharing in moments of joy	**confidence** in moments of doubt	**wonder** in moments of sadness

The best act statements reflect a level of tension, intensity, or urgency

And then we create acts. We ask:

Imagine if....

World Wildlife Fund Earth Hour

In just three years Earth Hour went from being an idea that motivated 2.2 million people in Sydney, Australia, to turn off the lights for an hour to show their concerns for climate change to a worldwide phenomenon that, in 2010, reached more than a billion people in 4,616 cities and towns in 129 countries switching off their lights to save the planet. Earth Hour, organized by the World Wildlife Fund (WWF), captured the world's collective consciousness: It was

the largest mass participation event in human history

– or any history, for that matter. Not bad for a brand whose purpose is to save the planet.

The human insight that drove the idea is that people want to make a positive difference but often feel that anything they do as individuals won't matter. But when hundreds of millions of individuals band together their action can inspire real change. Getting that unity of action, however, would demand a creative idea as powerful and compelling as the problem it was trying to solve.

So we had a real and deep insight into people and we had a profound historic purpose. What HumanKind act would be worthy? Could be worthy? The answer was the polar opposite in tone from the insight and purpose: neither deep nor historic, but certainly real. As simple as flipping a switch from on to off.

The brilliance is not just that Earth Hour made switching off the lights a symbolic act but that, in 2009, the act itself became a symbolic vote – and votes count!

By making their individual voices heard a collective voice would flow and large-scale government action would follow.

Villagers in Kenya participated in Earth Hour 2010 as did city dwellers in Kosovo and farmers in Kansas. United Nations Secretary-General, Ban Ki-moon, Al Gore, and Archbishop Desmond Tutu took part. So did Ashton Kutcher, Coldplay, Pedro Almodóvar, and Kylie Minogue; supermodel Gisele Bündchen and her husband, New England Patriots quarterback Tom Brady, among thousands of other sports figures, performers, writers, politicians, artists, and religious leaders. Some of the most famously lit places on earth went dark, including the Chrysler Building in New York, the Golden Gate Bridge in San Francisco, and even the welcome sign on the Las Vegas strip; the avenue bordering the Copacabana beach in Rio de Janeiro; the Fontana di Trevi in Rome; the Notre Dame in Paris; Big Ben, Buckingham Palace, and Number 10 Downing St. in London; the CN Tower in Toronto; and more than a thousand other world icons and heritage sites. Earth Hour was the number one topic on Twitter for most of the 24 hours.

Earth Hour was promoted in every way possible – in gripping television and radio spots, online, print ads, public relations, and even (separate from anything Leo Burnett did) with "eco-tinis" at bars in Phoenix and dollar-off coupons at Fish & Co., a fish 'n' chips restaurant chain in Singapore and Malaysia. This was participation and involvement in a brand like never before. Earth Hour truly became the people's cause.

Humankind took a HumanKind idea and ran with it, creating and recreating new acts that all encouraged the same thing. In the end, it was simply epic.

VOTE

EARTH!

Sydney

Cairo

Rio de Janeiro

Paris

London

Hong Kong

1 in 7 people were
reached by Earth Hour

A 2,000% increase in
participation from 2008

Over 4,000 cities
across 88 countries

V

Number one topic on
Twitter and YouTube on
the day of Earth Hour

Vote Earth Web site
received unique visits
from 212 countries

The campaign
reached the target of
over 1 billion people

In 2009, China, India and the Middle East took part for the first time

As a mandate for action 18 of the G20 countries, and 38 of the C40 cities voted Earth

1,059 of the world's icons voted Earth

s

87 million online mentions during the Vote Earth campaign

Coldplay held a carbon-neutral concert in support of Earth Hour

Google made the Earth Hour site available in 35 countries

YOUR LIGHT SWITCH

60 EARTH HOUR

IS YOUR VOTE

SWITCH OFF YOUR LIGHTS FOR EARTH HOUR
SATURDAY // MARCH 28, 8:30 - 9:30PM

L'INTERRUPTEUR

60 EARTH HOUR

C'EST TON VOTE

ÉTEIGNEZ VOS LUMIÈRES PENDANT EARTH HOUR
SAMEDI LE 28 MARS 20H30-21H30

开关

60 EARTH HOUR

就是你的选择

用关灯行动支持地球一小时
星期六//3月28日, 20:30-21:30

VOTE EARTH!

YOUR LIGHT SWITCH
IS YOUR VOTE

SWITCH OFF YOUR LIGHTS FOR EARTH HOUR
SATURDAY // MARCH 28, 8:30 - 9:30PM

VOTONS POUR

LA PLANÈTE!

ÉTEIGNEZ VOS LUMIÈRES PENDANT EARTH HOUR
SAMEDI LE 28 MARS 20H30-21H30

选择地球!

用关灯行动
支持地球一小时

星期六//3月28日, 20:30-21:30

VOTE!
EARTH

SWITCH OFF YOUR LIGHTS FOR EARTH HOUR
MARCH 28TH // 8:30 - 9:30PM

VOTA
POR EL
PLANETA!

APAGA LAS LUCES PARA LA HORA DEL PLANETA
SABADO 28 DE MARZO A LAS 8:30-9:30PM

选择地球!

用关灯行动支持地球一小时
星期六//3月28日, 20:30-21:30

earthhour.org

Using an integrated global campaign, Earth Hour was transformed from a symbol into a political mandate for action made possible by a vote that was not about what country you're from but, instead, what planet you're from.

Diageo's Pampero Rum Ephemeral Museum

When the mayor of Lisbon announced that he would whitewash walls throughout the city to rid them of graffiti and street art, little did he know that he would spur a movement, inspire an edgy, one-of-a-kind art happening, and help Diageo's Pampero rum build the street cred it needed to reach the fashion, art, and design crowd of Portugal's capital.

As it happens, until Pampero got involved, rum had a reputation as a drink for the older set. Moreover, the leading brand of rum had already been well-established in Portuguese society for 15 years. So Pampero not only had to update the reputation of rum itself, but also introduce its brand to an audience that wasn't that interested in the category.

Pampero and the Leo Burnett team in Lisbon knew its audience well enough to know that any sort of traditional advertising would fail to connect with the right people in the right way. After all, saying you're hip and actually being hip are vastly different propositions. Pampero had to invite participation in the brand in a way that the people it wanted to attract would take the time to appreciate and respect.

The mayor gave Pampero the perfect opening. It turned out that the majority of the graffiti and street art he planned to whitewash was in the Bairro Alto district, whose club-, gallery-, bar-, and boutique-lined streets attracted the people Pampero wanted to reach. What if Pampero, through its Pampero Fundación, could save the district's grafitti and street art by dubbing the streets a living, outdoor museum – the world's first "ephemeral" museum – where the art is here today and gone tomorrow? And so Museu Efémero was born.

First, the team scoured the district to identify what work was worth saving and what was merely vandalism. They met with all the artists they could locate to catalog the pieces, labeling them just as any museum would do. Then they made a street map with walking tours and an audio tour that visitors to the specially created Museu Efémero Web site could download onto their mp3 players. Soon, thanks to Pampero rum, thousands of people were walking around the district with headphones learning about the art on the walls.

In no time they realized they had a new kind of museum blockbuster on their hands – a grassroots cultural movement of which any major metropolitan museum would be proud. Museu Efémero attracted more visitors than most of the city's other, more traditional museums; notice from the city's print, television, and online media; and, incredibly, inclusion in tourist guides. The only attention Museu Efémero didn't get was from the mayor, who didn't say or *do* anything. Museu Efémero became so popular and well-known that Pampero rum matched its leading competitor in both awareness and sales.

Pampero followed up its Bairro Alto museum with "galleries" in São Bento and Amoreiras, two other hip Lisbon neighborhoods, and has plans for similar "ephemeral" museums in other world cities.

MUSEU EFÉMERO

EFEITO MAGENTA
Love Project · Stencil

WWW.MUSEUEFEMERO.COM | TRACK 8:

Graffiti dominates the streets of Lisbon's historic Bairro Alto district. With Leo Burnett's help, Pampero rum became the official tour guide for all the art suffusing the neighborhood's walls.

Heineken Stadium of Dreams

It's hard to imagine how the frenzied excitement over the Union of European Football Associations (UEFA) Champions League matches and the launch of a new beer can could ever compete. One involves the most popular sport on the planet, millions if not billions of fans, and media attention around the globe. The other involves a can.

And yet when challenged by Heineken in Bangkok to use its new, limited-edition can to promote the brand's sponsorship of the league, the love affair between the Thai people and the game of football inspired Leo Burnett to connect them both, on a massive scale, to Heineken.

The plan for the can was that after the championship match, its final score would be imprinted on the new design, which would then be sold after the game's end, turning the can into a keepsake. The problem was that while the championship built excitement and anticipation, leading up the final match, there was no commensurate build up to the launch of the can itself. That is, until the team dreamed up the idea of uniting everyone's dream of winning in one place – a "Stadium of Dreams" built entirely from Heineken cans. Thousands of cans. Tens of thousands of cans. *Hundreds of thousands* of cans.

The idea wasn't for Heineken to build the stadium, however, but for football (and Heineken) fans to do it by going to a specially created Web site to virtually place a can on the construction site as a mason might a real brick. In fact, these virtual masons were able to see the blueprint for the stadium and choose the exact spot to place their can, joining with other people to build the stadium and share their love of the game.

As the actual stadium was being built in the center of Bangkok they could even visit and see the can they chose. Dozens of ads and banners, intense media attention, and word of mouth drove people to the Stadium of Dreams Web site – 332,654 cans worth of people, in fact. It also drove thousands of people to gather live at the Stadium of Dreams to watch and share in the excitement of each week's match on huge video screens that hung from its side.

Ultimately, the Stadium of Dreams created interest around and involvement in what is normally a very dull thing – a new can – by dramatizing the relationship between Heineken and football and inviting the Thai people to bring the action to life. The wait for the new can became as exciting as the wait for the final match, which resulted in Futbol Club Barcelona 2-0 Manchester United, a score eventually imprinted on the historic, limited-edition can.

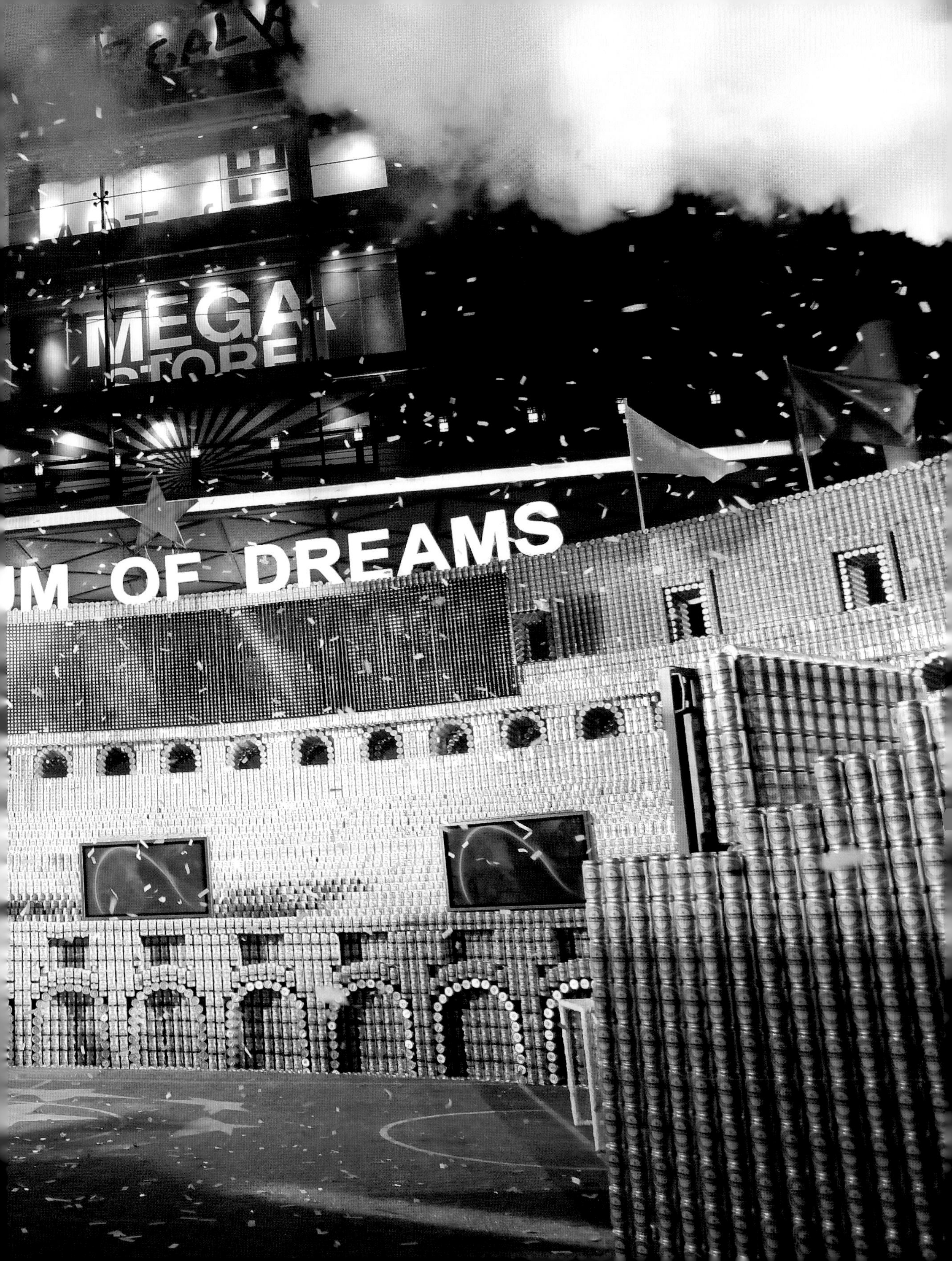

MEGA
STORE
UM OF DREAMS

In the end, it all came down to this –
Heineken cans with the match's final
score imprinted on them.

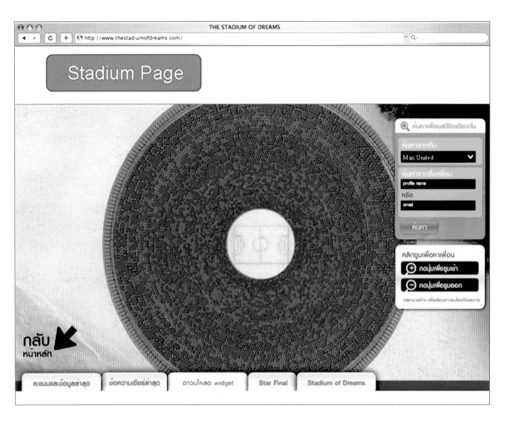

Canon Photochains

Products crammed with features can easily fall into the habit of being about nothing more than their features. You know, the whole my-feature-is-bigger-than-your-feature thing. The problem is, in any particular category, individual brands can only be a feature leader for so long. Every competitor within a category is feverishly working on the same things, trying every day to out-feature the next guy. After a while it's Sisyphean – pushing that rock up the hill, creating that hot new feature, only to have the rock roll down the hill again, only to have to create another new feature to outpace everyone else.

So, for certain kinds of products working to identify a human brand purpose, overlooking features – or at least setting them aside – can be a colossal challenge. You think of Canon, for instance, and you think cameras. And features, lots of features. But Canon looked beyond its features, its R&D group, and the folks who live to experience the slightest refinement or addition, to what the whole Canon experience is really about. To identify Canon's authentic *human* purpose.

Taking pictures? You bet. But *only* taking pictures? *Hardly.*

Moonlight

Black & White

Everything

Sky

Two

These photochains are a novel form
of social networking for photographers,
in which each image contains a single
detail that serves as the inspiration
point for the next photograph.

Walk   Color & Beauty   Window   Around the World   Hero

JUMP

Canon is about creative expression. About opportunity to articulate through imagery what you feel, how you view the world, the wisdom you've gained along the way, the unique way you see things. Just as those prehistoric cave dwellers' drawing of animals in Lascaux are about more than merely depicting animals, photographers' pictures are about more than merely depicting what they see in front of them. For many it's about what's in their mind's eye. Tap into that insight and you see a human brand purpose bloom within.

Canon figured this out, which is why its "Photochain" campaign for its EOS brand made such an immediate and extraordinary connection in Asia-Pacific, especially Australia where it was created in our Sydney office. Rooted in the brand and true to how people communicate and share information in the 21st century, Canon "Photochain" is an innovative twist on the dynamic of social networking. It invited participation in a way that allowed people to connect, create, and cause others to feel inspired, perhaps the greatest gift a creative person can receive. It was true to the brand's purpose, however

unstated that purpose remained to the everyday photographer.

Like the best ideas, "Photochain" is simple: It invites people to take a picture, tag its details – a color, a shape, an object, even a feeling – and post it. Others see it. They feel inspired. They take a picture, tag it and post it. Someone now sees this second picture and, inspired, takes, tags, and posts their own photo. And a photochain is born.

A fully interactive experience based solely on an individual's wish to participate and connect, the campaign included a national

television spot, direct mail, and a Web site, all driving people to become inspired, become involved, and connect with a community of photographers. The idea created loyal fans and an intimacy with the brand and other users that was at once different yet familiar – a new feeling but one that was completely natural.

Canon "Photochain" not only invited creative participation but built HumanKind populism, moving Canon one step further to becoming more than a highly successful global brand, but one sustained by people. A people's brand.

This spot shows the Canon photochain in action, as well as the HumanKind interaction Canon invited its fans to join: After the first person uploads a picture to the site, other people take their inspiration from it – maybe an object (box!) or color (orange!) or action (flying!) – and shoot their own photos. They, too, upload their photos and on and on creating

a chain of photos that brings to life the idea that Canon is about more than cameras; Canon is about creative expression and 21ˢᵗ-century-style sharing. This campaign was designed to generate participation and stimulate people's imaginations, while differentiating Canon from its competitors as a brand focused on cultivating human connections.

Kronenbourg 1664 Can-Camera

Given beer's ubiquity among drinkers, generating interest in beer (let alone a beer can) takes breakthrough thinking on a scale almost as big as Russia. As it turns out, Kronenbourg 1664 thinks big. Research showed that the edgy, arty crowd the brand hoped to reach in, of all places, Russia – especially Russian men – were always on the lookout for new ways to express themselves creatively, which dovetailed perfectly with the historic link between the brand and the world of art.

With this insight, we realized that while a can is a can is a can, a can can also be a camera – a can-camera based on the principle of *camera obscura* – that would give Kronenbourg drinkers the opportunity to actually use the can to produce art. Not only would the can-camera allow people to create rich imagery, but it would reward them for their participation with a new and truly unique way to express themselves.

To dramatize and humanize the can-camera, we asked renowned French photographer Michel Setboun to use it to take photographs of his beloved Paris. The pictures he took of the Louvre, the Seine, and other Paris landmarks caught the imagination of the people more than a thousand miles away in Moscow, so much so that Kronenbourg hosted a standing-room-only exhibition of Setboun's can-camera work there. Instructions online that showed people how to create their own can-camera gave thousands of would-be DIY Russian photographers the chance to create their own camera, their own art, and highly personal associations with the brand which, ultimately, lead to a sold-out stock of limited-edition cans two months earlier than anticipated.

More importantly, the can-camera was an application of HumanKind thinking that altered how people thought about the Kronenbourg brand (it's a great alternative to vodka), what it allowed them to accomplish (more than just relax), how it provided an opportunity for artistic expression (cool photographs) and, of course, how they behaved (they purchased it).

When French photographer Michel Setboun, whose work has appeared in *The New York Times, Life, Paris Match, Stern,* and *Le Figaro,* used his Kronenbourg 1664 can-camera to capture the sights of Paris, the beautiful and moody pictures he took showcased the city as never before.

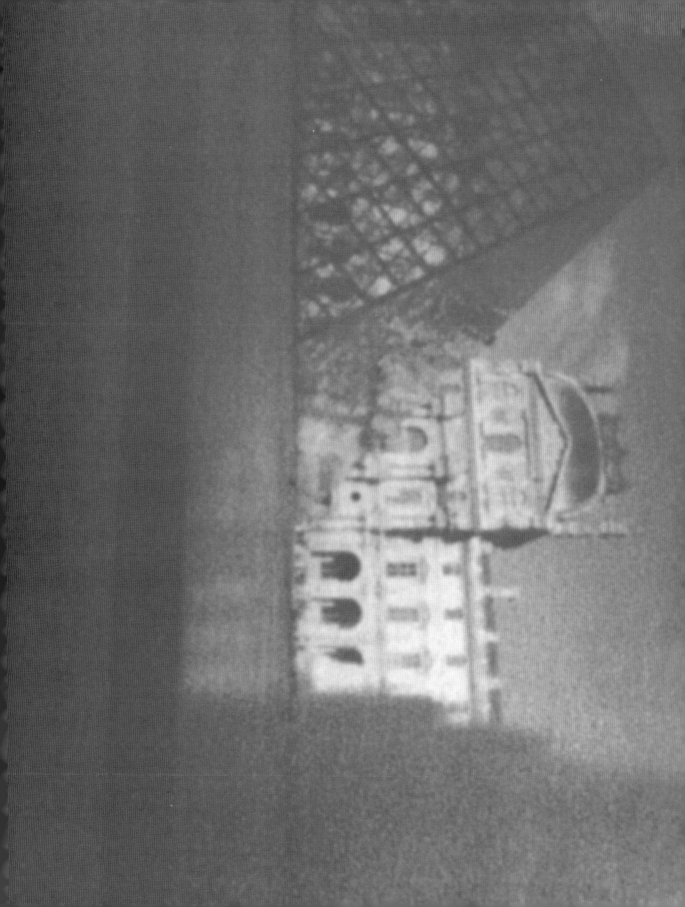

Populism

Imaginative Populism

In a world increasingly obsessed with niche communication, in a world in which marketing can be a one-to-one thing, in a world where marketing practices are increasingly fragmented, in that world we say, uh-uh, hang on, there's still this power of mass, and there's still this joy – yes, *joy* – in doing mass marketing.

Getting people to take up Sports Slurping for Slurpee in Australia.

Rallying beer drinkers to promote Man's Day for Bergenbier in Romania.

Persuading sports fans to create the Stadium of Dreams out of thousands of beer cans for Heineken in Bangkok.

Captivating commuters with fresh salads that are growing on billboards along the highway for McDonald's in Chicago.

Encouraging people to literally purchase hope at the Red Cross store in Lisbon.

But that joy, and successful mass marketing, isn't easy to achieve. That's why HumanKind is so important. It provides a context, a language, and a compendium of ideas that have allowed us at Leo Burnett to think similarly no matter where in the world we are (or what language we think in) and to share a way of approaching our work that helps brands communicate and interact with the world honestly and authentically.

HumanKind says that by continually studying and forming new insights into people, people will respond.

HumanKind says that by using your insight into people and human needs to uncover a brand's human purpose, people will respond.

HumanKind says that by using that purpose as inspiration for acts that allow for participation, people will respond.

And HumanKind says that if you move from people to purpose to participation, you will reach what we call brand populism. You will create an environment in which a brand can emerge as a "people's brand."

Earth Hour
the people's movement

Nintendo
the people's game

McDonald's
the people's restaurant

Fiat
the people's car

Kellogg's
the people's cereal

Coke
the people's drink

Brand populism is what comes from a HumanKind approach and belief in the unifying power of mass marketing. Work inspired by human brand purpose can weave a brand into people's lives so much so that the brand itself becomes a part of the social fabric. The value of the brand to society becomes equal to the value of society to the brand. It's hard to imagine the world without McDonald's or Kellogg's cereal.

It isn't commercials or print ads or posters or Web sites or radio spots or short films or viral videos or Facebook pages or Twitter streams or mobile apps or coupons or concerts or celebrities or tag lines or jingles or any other form of communications that create great, life-affirming, enjoyable, meaningful, valuable, iconic people's brands. It's people who do.

Creativity can transform human behavior. We've seen it in action. We've seen the results. We've seen people become the force behind and sustenance of people's brands. By applying a HumanKind approach we give brands and people the opportunity to exchange ideas and value so they both benefit.

Imagination is the currency of what we do, brand populism is the result.

value of
the brand
to society

=

value of
society to
the brand

It's not easy for once-popular brands to reclaim their former glory, especially if that brand, like Fiat, had been an iconic symbol of freedom, optimism, and, of course, *la dolce vita*. But that was the challenge Fiat faced when it planned to reintroduce the brand's automotive legend, the Fiat 500, in Italy in 2007 – exactly 50 years after its original launch.

To take what had been the original "people's car" and recreate it once again as a car for the adventurous, young-at-heart drivers of today, Fiat needed to reignite the Italian people's love, passion, and respect for the brand by connecting with them in a new and modern way.

Fiat 500's human brand purpose of "existing to supply great, joyful little cars for people made by people" led naturally to the "500 Wants You" campaign, which kicked off 500 days before the car hit the streets. "500 Wants You" invited people to visit the online concept lab's virtual configurator to design and choose the features of *their* perfect Fiat 500. At the same time they were creating their own car, they were also be contributing to the re-creation of a new national icon that would define their generation just as the original defined its generation a half-century earlier.

Site visitors could choose and suggest accessories, textures, materials, graphics, fabrics, and technologies. When the colors for the car originally proposed by Fiat didn't excite or inspire the 500 Wants You site visitors, who suggested a much more vibrant color selection, Fiat nixed its plans and offered a far more vivid palette. Given the number of ways people were able to design their own cars and combine features,

500,000 Fiat 500s could have been lined up in a row and no two would be alike.

The campaign expanded to include many ways people could engage with the brand and participate above and beyond the design element – by contributing to 500-ology, a massive online encyclopedia of stories and pictures dedicated to the 500; entering a design contest for students and professionals with Giorgio Armani as one of the judges; and even by supplying ideas for the Fiat site's redesign and for a brand logo and mascot.

Over the course of the 500 days, as world-wide media attention snowballed (*The Sun* newspaper called the Fiat 500 "the must-have motor for fashion-conscious supermini buyers") and more than 3.5 million people contributed their ideas, the Fiat 500 truly became the people's car. No need existed to dub it that, or to advertise it as such. It was the people's car naturally once again. Fiat had created

the most widespread interaction between a car and its potential buyers in history.

No longer were people passive recipients in a car's creation; instead they became active participants in it – people actually creating the new people's car.

And, even better for the brand, only eight weeks after its launch, 80,000 vehicles were ordered, more than half the forecasted target for the entire first year.

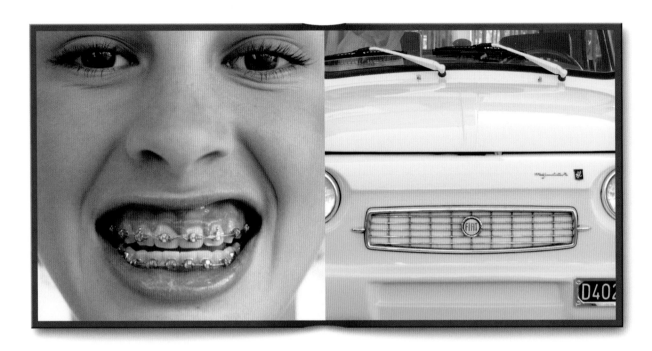

The first car for the people, created by the people

Fiat invited potential Fiat 500 buyers to design their own cars and their response inspired an extraordinary outpouring of creativity, not only showcasing the car but the value of HumanKind itself.

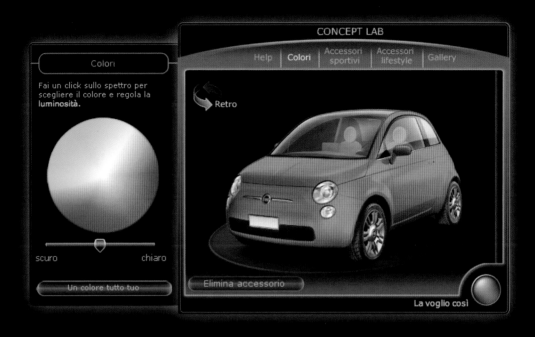

NikeiD. Generator

Fukuoka, a city of 1.5 million people about 900 kilometers (560 miles) from Tokyo, is home to some of Japan's fiercest trendsetters. They've seen it all, they've done it all, they've even worn it all. So when Nike opened a three-story flagship store there, it knew that it had to offer a creative in-store experience every bit as cool and unique as those it hoped to attract or the store would become passé right away.

That the city's young fashionistas craved any opportunity to personalize their look dovetailed perfectly with Nike's human brand purpose, however, so we created the NikeiD. Generator, a proprietary, interactive, digital, color-analyzing camera that invited people to participate in both the Nike brand and their own invention by designing the hottest one-of-a-kind shoes they could imagine.

A person stood in front of the NikeiD. Generator camera on the store's ground floor and took their own picture, which magically transformed the colors of their clothes into color particles, which then served as the color palette in a real-time custom shoe design, a photo of which each person was

given. By changing clothes or adding colors, new designs could be generated until the perfect pair of shoes was created. (The design would then be printed onto a sticker at the store's NikeiD. Studio.)

Beautiful in its simplicity, high-tech in its execution, and tailored to a savvy, fashion-conscious crowd that appreciates customization, prizes creative expression, and expects technological inventiveness, the NikeiD. Generator attracted 18,000 people during the store's four-day grand opening, with 95 percent of those who designed their own shoes moving through the store to its third floor, which housed the NikeiD. Studio.

NIKEiD.GE

NERATOR

キミスペシャル完成。

NikeFukuoka ✓

Your iD Number
25A83

NikeiD. Generator allowed Fukuoka's
trendsetters to design their own Nikes,
involving them in the creative process
in a new and unique way.

Bergenbier Man's Day

By 2007, Bergenbier had a real challenge on its hands. Beer communications has traditionally been tied to taste, sports, ritual, and sex – tried and true conceits, perhaps, yet pretty tired. But as the country's number one beer in a country of just 22 million where more than 30 beers vie for people's attention, additional everyday advertising wasn't going to break through. It was an atmosphere perfect for HumanKind's push for "acts, not ads," to break through by breaking through the limiting nature of conventional beer advertising.

Research produced a key, double-whammy insight into Romanian men, who are Bergenbier's biggest drinkers. First, men didn't have a holiday to call their own (not even a Father's Day). Second, Romania was among the European countries with the fewest number of holidays. Put those two facts together and you can see the problem. So the big question became what could *we* do to help Bergenbier help men feel the love? Once we began to think about the challenge through a human lens, we formed this insight into the deficit among Romania's male population and saw an obvious, if uphill, solution. Create a day for men. Create Man's Day, an annual national holiday. And have Bergenbier lead the charge.

But anyone, or any brand, or any beer, can say today is Man's Day. We wanted the Romanian *parliament* to say it, to proclaim it by law. Only then would people celebrate the holiday, hopefully, or course, by toasting the day with a couple of chilled Bergenbiers.

And here's where the "act" began that invited people to participate. After all, Bergenbier couldn't get the government to act, but Bergenbier – the *people's* beer – could provide the means by which the *people* could get the government to act.

The campaign to institute a Man's Day in Romania inspired a national spectacle, kickstarted and sustained by a cheeky Web site that asked men why they deserved a Man's Day. More than 1,900 responses were posted ("because our national football team loses," "because we've been in the army," "because we go bald"), many of which were then turned into highly anticipated commercials and print ads. Finally, an actual piece of legislation was drawn up for the government to consider, which attracted more than 425,000 supporting signatures from the Romanian people.

The campaign caught the media's attention, too, which covered its every angle and generated hundreds of print articles, online features and comments, and television news spots. "They want a day just for them…" one news anchor said on the nightly news. "Men don't want to be deprived of such a privilege."

An integrated advertising campaign, a compelling and interactive online presence, dedicated Bergenbier packaging, flags, posters, campaign material, and a massive event that attracted tens of thousands of people, were all a part of the act of getting parliament to take up and vote for Man's Day.

While the Romanian parliament never took the bait and voted on the legislation, as far as Romanian men were concerned – the people, after all – the campaign was a huge success. A brand invited mass participation in its communications and a new holiday had entered mass culture as a result. Now millions of men congratulate one another on their day with the knowledge that their favorite brand of beer created for them something meaningful and authentic – something beyond advertising, something real. A day to call their own.

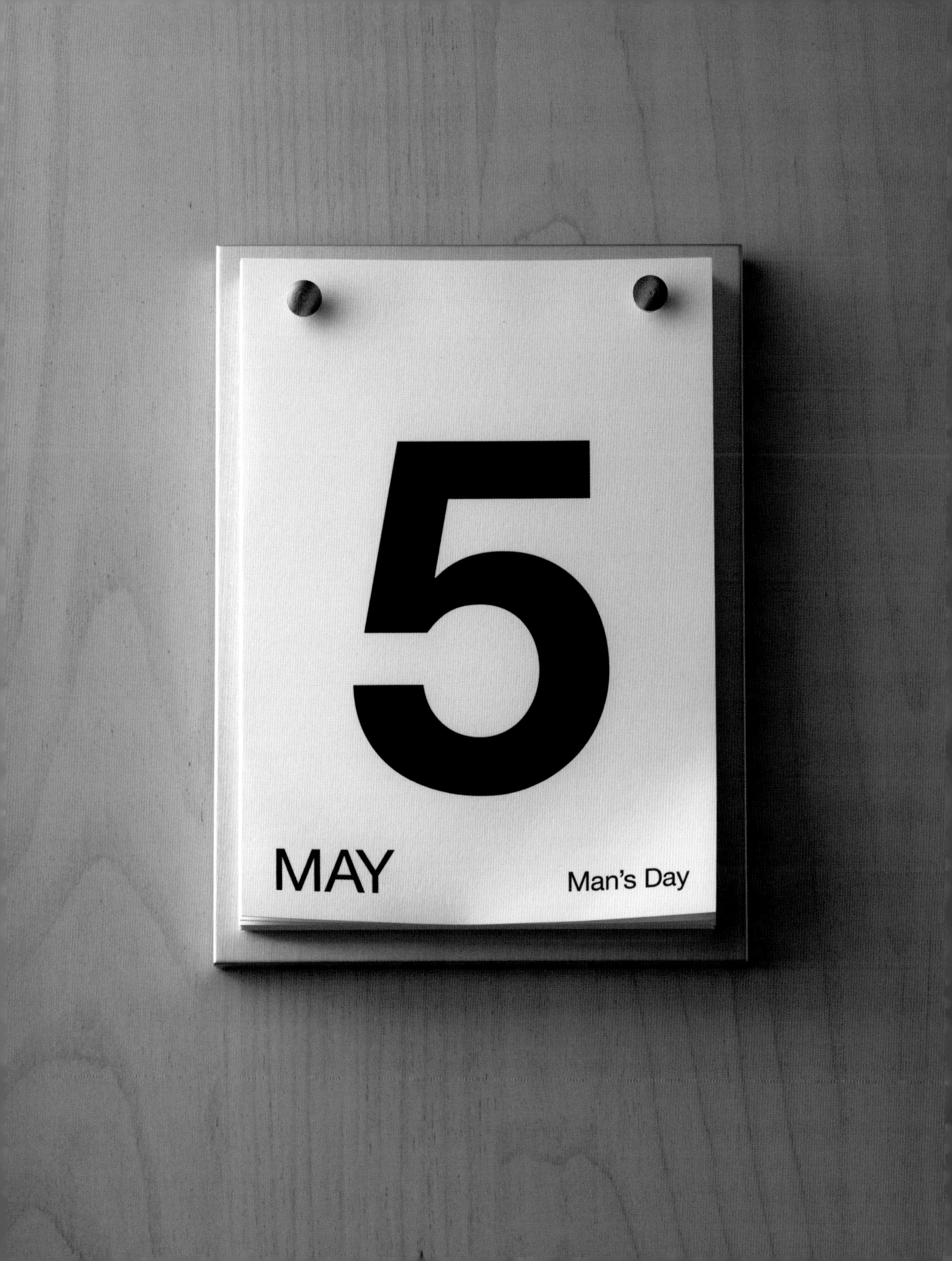
5
MAY
Man's Day

James Ready Share Our Billboard

Advertising is expensive, we know. So one of our clients, the Canadian micro-brewery James Ready beer, decided to make this fact central to its communications, which made sense because the whole thing about James Ready is that it's a discount lager. Not counting Canadian taxes, it's a buck a bottle. People like that, especially younger people. That's its thing. A buck a bottle.

But a buck doesn't go very far these days. So as we worked with James Ready we identified its human purpose: James Ready exists to help you enjoy life for less. Not only that, but it cedes some control over that to you. You get to decide in a way because James Ready says you do. And it exists to give you the opportunity to have some say in just how cheap the company can keep its beer.

James Ready already had a reputation for asking its loyal customers to get involved, from returning bottle caps and labels to volunteering as beer girls. So it made sense then when James Ready announced that it couldn't pay for an elaborate advertising campaign and asked these same loyal customers to do even more. To, in a way, get famous for James Ready's benefit.

That's where "Help Keep James Ready a Buck" came in: It asked people to share its billboard space.

To show the love.

The campaign started with a simple call for help. In newspaper ads – only the cheap spaces, of course. Through personal e-mails to drinkers. Via the James Ready newsletter. Billboards also appeared around Southern Ontario that said HELP KEEP JAMES READY A BUCK. SHARE OUR BILLBOARD. MAKE

US AN OFFER AT JAMESREADY.COM. Sure, it was a pretty traditional billboard, but the request wasn't. It invited people to participate and co-create with the brand in a fresh new way.

People were directed to a Web site where they could make an offer for the billboard spaces – not an offer of money, but one of a message or image that could be featured on a James Ready billboard. It didn't take long for James Ready's fans to respond. Images flooded in.

True to its word, James Ready used those images and the sentiments that accompanied them on 106 billboards plastered throughout the region with the tag line THANKS FOR KEEPING J.R. A BUCK. (Actually, it was more personal than that. The billboards said things like THANKS NIKKI FOR KEEPING J.R. A BUCK. THANKS JOSH FOR KEEPING J.R. A BUCK. THANKS LAYLA FOR KEEPING J.R., A BUCK.) The brand struck a HumanKind chord with James Ready's customers because the request was authentic to what James Ready is and has always been. The brand didn't have to come out and say "this is our human purpose." Its communications communicated its purpose.

People got it.

Better yet – for both the beer and its fans – the folks in the billboards became famous, at least locally. People recognized them on the street. Local media profiled them. People talked about them. They became brand spokespeople, but the best kind of spokespeople because they were just being themselves. And they were people who just so happened to love James Ready beer.

Best dog ever!

THANKS EMILY FOR KEEPING J.R. A BUCK.

Ready to come home!

THANKS MIKE FOR KEEPING J.R. A BUCK.

Sir James Ready on Hallowe'en

THANKS SAMUEL FOR KEEPING J.R. A BUCK.

Don't worry ... CFJ Knockle is not invited!

THANKS SONNY FOR KEEPING J.R. A BUCK.

R U READY!!

THANKS NATASHA FOR KEEPING J.R. A BUCK.

Rideau Ricochets

THANKS NICKY FOR KEEPING J.R. A BUCK.

Always Ready

THANKS MATTHEW FOR KEEPING J.R. A BUCK.

2nd Annual Wildcats Alumni Game "Get Ready Boys" - June 12th

THANKS KEVIN FOR KEEPING J.R. A BUCK.

THANKS ANDY FOR KEEPING J.R. A BUCK.

Ready to tie the knot

THANKS TRACY & DEAN FOR KEEPING J.R. A BUCK.

"Hi Mom & Dad!"

THANKS JON & NAT FOR KEEPING J.R. A BUCK.

THANKS CORY FOR KEEPING J.R. A BUCK.

THANKS GALS FOR KEEPING J.R. A BUCK.

THANKS SHAWN FOR KEEPING J.R. A BUCK.

THANKS CORY FOR KEEPING J.R. A BUCK.

Ad age don't c iconic l people

ncies
reate
brands,
do

When we say that HumanKind can contribute to making advertising a nobler profession, we aren't pretending that HumanKind is going to save the word (even if it helps some of our clients save the world). Instead, we mean that HumanKind can lead to a more honest and compelling and rewarding communion between brands and people, and that, in and of itself, is good.

We need more honesty in the world, and more relationships built on a foundation of trust, authenticity, respect, and purpose, no matter who – or what – they are between. HumanKind can help build that world.

HumanKind is an approach to communications that we believe is true to who we are, and who we have always been, and true to the way we want to conduct business and what we as a company and as individuals want to accomplish.

And our clients think so, too. From the big multinational players to the little guy down the block, they, like us, believe that…

understanding and continually deepening our collective insight into people…

using that insight to uncover and celebrate a brand purpose rooted in genuine and fundamental human need…

and imaginatively activating that purpose to invite meaningful and enjoyable participation in their brand communications…

can lead to brand populism and to becoming a "people's brand."

And that brand populism will both sustain their business and help people live better lives, whether enjoying a simple meal with their families or, yes, saving the world.

We believe in the power of creativity to transform human behavior.

People
Purpose
Participation
Populism

Welcome to
HumanKind

When a brand is purpose-inspired, meaningful acts... bring that purpose to life

Marc Pritchard
Global Chief Marketing Officer
P&G

Purpose

When a brand is purpose-inspired, meaningful acts that touch the hearts of people are often one of the best ways to bring that purpose to life. For example, the purpose of Pampers is to care for the happy, healthy development of babies. Pampers provides diapers with outstanding dryness and comfort so baby can sleep, play, and explore – and so develop in a healthy way. And Pampers also acts to care for babies around the world, too, with "UNICEF ONE PACK = ONE VACCINE." For every pack of Pampers purchased, one vaccine is sent to vaccinate babies from neonatal tetanus. Pampers literally saves the lives of babies around the world – a great example of bringing purpose to life.

Mark Baynes
Global Chief Marketing Officer
Kellogg's Company

Mary Dillon
Global Chief Marketing Officer
McDonald's Corporation

Joe Tripodi
EVP, Chief Marketing and Commercial Officer
The Coca-Cola Company

Body Image

Women's desire to achieve happiness through their weight begins with a journey that is anything but happy. She says she doesn't want a quick fix, she wants a life change, but she is more likely to end up describing it as a life sentence. And yet she stays optimistic because she remembers what it feels like to win the struggle, a win that is about more than just a number on a scale. We've heard women say "when I look good, I feel good." It's about more than just the weight she loses, its about the confidence she gains – confidence that in and of itself improves her appearance through her overall attitude and even behavior.

Branding

Ray Kroc always said we are the "people's brand" and more than 50 years after we were founded, we continue to believe that. When McDonald's has done well over its history it's because we were listening to our customers. When we have not done as well, it's because we were not listening as carefully. We ask our people around the world – as we consider our products, our promotions, our place, our pricing – to think about a very simple question: how can we provide the simplest, easiest, and most enjoyable experience for people? As my colleague Matt Biespiel, our director of global brand strategy, notes, "That's what drives everything that we do."

Creativity

We work on two levels. We're working on the physical satisfaction of refreshment, and then the emotional satisfaction of delivering what we think is happiness. And we apply creativity to these two things in different ways depending on where in the world we're working. In less developed markets, like China and India, we're less conceptual, more literal, and think about how to creatively make the brand's intrinsic benefits visible to people. But in other parts of the world, we move beyond the physical satisfaction of our product and let the emotional satisfaction of delivering what we believe is happiness drive our creativity.

Lisa Cochrane
Vice President of Marketing
Allstate Corporation

Security

Let's face it, insurance was never what you'd call a people-friendly business. It was always about the actuaries, the lawyers, the big companies and their agents. As an "insured" you were not a person, you were a policy holder, a VIN number. Today we are reinventing the insurance industry by giving insurance a human face. We're making real the active protection that it provides people. Life is full of risks and uncertainties – some good, some bad. Working with HumanKind means understanding how we can better ensure safety and security in a people-centered way. This brings us to our fundamentally human brand purpose: *We exist to actively protect people from life's uncertainties, every day.*

Andy Ridley
Executive Director
Earth Hour Global

Participation

Whether you're a nonprofit or a for-profit brand, reaching people has to be about painting a picture of the future and projecting a vision of how you want it to be. People want to be told what's possible and how to improve their life, even if that just means a great meal for dinner tonight or, more importantly, a great world for your kids in the future. Reaching people and communicating with them from a place of hope is always more fruitful than reaching them through fear. Humans are essentially positive, and to speak to them as if that's not the case is a disservice not only to them but to your brand.

Ashish Banerjee
Vice President of Branding
du

Communication

Brands must revolve around people, because people produce, propel, and purchase brands. The people who run the successful brands of our time know this well. They make their brands reach out to people, because they know that brands must embrace people before people will embrace them. Contemporary practice and discourse should not be about "branding," which is outside-in and superficial, much like the effect of wrought-iron symbols on cattle. Instead, marketers must focus on brand development to build better brands from the inside-out, based on a philosophical view of the brand, its reason for being, its place and role in the world, and its stance towards people.

Rebecca Brock
Brand Controller
Homebase

Giovanni Perosino
Communication Director
Fiat International Group

Reggie Fils-Aime
President and Chief Operating Officer
Nintendo of America Inc.

Home

The home improvement category "does what it says on the tin" – it allows people to improve the quality of their homes and therefore their lives. The role that home plays in our lives, no matter how modest or grand that home, cannot be overstated. A home is not just the four walls in which you live, not just a space to which you return to every day. It is *the* place that allows you to be you. It reflects you and your lifestyle because it is entirely yours, defined, chosen and created by you. It is a place of security that offers emotional as well as functional comfort. It becomes a place of stability because you made it that way.

People

Five years ago when Fiat was sitting on the verge of disaster and began its reconstruction process, we decided that we could go back to listening to people, like we did in 1957 with the first 500, or we could close the shop and go home. In other words, we asked ourselves exactly why we exist. The answer? We exist to give people cars that are smaller, engines that are cleaner, and good design that is not for the few. It is for all. If I found myself today in the situation we had five years ago, with a brand in crisis, I wouldn't hesitate for a minute: go back to people, go back to HumanKind.

Play

As adults we're supposed to give up playing. But at Nintendo we see a world where play isn't something that ends when you "grow up," but something you embrace throughout life's journey. We believe playing enhances the human condition; we believe in a world view that says everything is possible. Objects on your desk suddenly transform into wondrous items of imagination. The view from your window begins to look like a playground. Play fuels our creativity, fires our imagination, enlightens our responsibility to ourselves and others, fosters our compassion, and builds our confidence. We look for endlessly magical ways to unlock the potential of play. Play just makes us better at life.

Like HumanKind itself, this book would not have been possible without the support of our clients and contribution of everyone at Leo Burnett, whose commitment to using creativity to transform human behavior has been boundless. We want to especially acknowledge several individuals who helped create this book; their creativity has helped transform these pages into a unique reflection of HumanKind

Mitsushi Abe
Rebecca Adams
Fuad Ahmad
Kaleem Bakurally
Jay Benjamin
Howard Bjornson
Debbie Bougdanos
Janice Capewell
Colleen Capola
Michael Canning
Chris Carlock
Manuela Colombini*
Alexandra Compain Tissier
Annette Corcoran
John Dada*
Andy DiLallo
Megan Emish
Alex Everett
Shepard Fairey
Mitchell Ferguson
Carol Foley
Jason Frohlichstein*
Rosalie Geier
Reza Ghanty
Anthony Gibson*
Jill Glickstein
Britt Godsell
Linda Goldberg*
Karen Green
M.G. Harti*
Giles Hedger
Andre Kirkelis*
Nikki Klimek*
Ben Kline

Donna Kopec
Atsuko Kubota
George Longley*
Alison McConnell
Jason McKean*
Marina Moraes
Lisa Morch
Ranil Nalawansa*
Milos Obradovic*
Christine Oliver
Nickay Penado
Shereen Peterson
Pia Pica
Chacho Puebla
Erick Rosa
Todd Sampson
Dan Santow
Michael Shanahan
Dani Simonds
Jennifer Skidgel
Barry Smith
Sompat Trisadikun*
Michael Wade
Annie Watson-Johnson
Drew Wehrle
Alisa Wolfson

A special thanks to those people who supplied images of humanity
from around the globe for the opening section of our book (*)

HumanKind

Published in the United States
by powerHouse Books
a division of powerHouse Cultural Entertainment, Inc.

37 Main Street, Brooklyn, NY 11201-1021
telephone: 212.604.9074 *fax:* 212.366.5247
email: humankind@powerhousebooks.com
website: www.powerhousebooks.com

First edition, 2010
Library of Congress Control Number: 2010929932
Hardcover ISBN 978-1-57687-549-0
Printing and binding by RR Donnelly, China
Book design by Leo Burnett, Chicago

A complete catalog of powerHouse Books
and Limited Editions is available upon request;
please call, write, or visit our website.

10 9 8 7 6 5 4 3 2 1

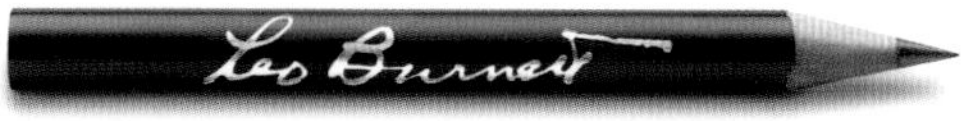
Leo Burnett